Itineraries around
MADRID
Routes and Trips

Itineraries around
MADRID
Routes and Trips

Luis Miguel Fraile Llorente

EDICIONES LA LIBRERÍA

To Carmen, Maite, Santiago, Juan, Blanca, Pilar, Sagrario, César, Félix, Mercedes, Nieves, María Teresa, Alicia, Guillermo, Raquel, Camelia and...to every person and company that collaborated in the promotion of my first book

In gratitude, I dedicate to them this third book.

© 2004, Luis Miguel Fraile Llorente
© 2004, Ediciones La Librería
C/ Mayor, 80
28013 MADRID
Telf.: 91 541 71 70
Fax: 91 548 93 93
info@edicioneslalibreria.com

Traducción: María Goicoechea
Fotografías: Luis Miguel Fraile Llorente
Portada y maquetación: Equipo de Diseño de Ediciones La Librería

Impresión: Gráficas Omnia
Encuadernación: Guijarro

I.S.B.N.: 84-95889-71-4
Depósito Legal: M-8015-2004

Contents

Presentation 11

Itineraries around the city of Madrid 13
  1. From Paseo del Pintor Rosales to Calle de Bailén 15
  2. From Plaza de la Encarnación to Cuesta de la Vega 23
  3. From Plaza de San Andrés to Calle de Segovia 31
  4. From Paseo de la Virgen del Puerto to Paseo de la Florida .. 37
  5. From Calle de la Princesa to Calle de Toledo 43
  6. From Calle de O'Donnell to Paseo de Recoletos 53
  7. From Plaza de Colón to Calle de Lope de Vega 63
  8. From Calle de Santa Isabel to Plaza de Murillo 69
  9. From Paseo del Prado to Puerta del Sol 75

Routes and trips around the Community of Madrid 83
  10. From Buitrago del Lozoya to Cotos 85
  11. San Lorenzo de El Escorial 93
  12. From Chinchón to Aranjuez 101
  13. Alcalá de Henares 109
  14. From Navacerrada to Manzanares El Rea 115

Trip to Toledo 119
  15. Toledo 121

Practical Data 131

Presentation

Madrid, a big cosmopolitan city always open to the traveller, is famous for its hospitality; that is why many visits become long, and even life-long, stays, as it is implied by the saying which better summarises the welcoming character of the city: "From Madrid to Heaven".

Madrid is a city loaded with History, with old conventual temples in whose stoned façades our past is engraved, ancient palaces, charmed spaces such as the Plaza Mayor, which has served as a model for so many others, or the Plaza de Oriente, which delicately caresses the immense granitic mass of the Royal Palace.

One cannot say to know Madrid if he or she has not traversed it from north to south and from east to west, if one has not entered the old churches built by men smitten with faith; if one has not walked along the labyrinth of primitive and twisted streets which were once the scenario for characters such as Cervantes, Lope de Vega, Calderón de la Barca, Velázquez, Goya and so many others that have contributed to write the history of our city; if one has not walked inside a tavern of the old Madrid and smelled the sweet scent oozed by its walls, so many were the glasses of wined drunk within them.

And if all this were not enough, the Community of Madrid has many places that are worth visiting, cities such as Alcalá de Henares or Aranjuez, both declared World Heritage, the Monastery of El Escorial, the Castle of Manzanares El Real, the Guadarrama Sierra, among others.

This book is an invitation to start travelling and getting to know our History, our capital's past and present, and that of its towns and of the most outstanding places of our Community, such as the neighbouring city of Toledo, also World Heritage and a compulsory visit for everyone who wants to know Madrid.

Itineraries around the city of Madrid

From Paseo del Pintor Rosales to Calle de Bailén

A very famous sentence says «From Madrid to heaven», so let us use this saying to begin our route.

Teleférico (cable railway) de la Casa de Campo

Facing number forty four of Paseo del Pintor Rosales (Parque de la Rosaleda) we find the famous cableway of Madrid, which offers us the possibility of enjoying wonderful (aerial) views of the first itinerary of this guide. A 2,5-kilometer walk takes us from Rosales to Casa de Campo and back. The view as we pass over the Manzanares River, and we see the highway M-30 about forty meters below our feet, is outstanding. At the Casa de Campo terminal it is possible

to make a stop and use the return ticket later.

Casa de Campo

Even if less well kept than the Retiro Park, the Casa de Campo is the biggest park of Madrid (1725 hectares –4,262.475 acres–). In the past, it was used as a private game preserve for the royalty. For a few decades now the park belongs to the people of Madrid, and it is one of the most visited places to enjoy a nice day outdoors. In the Casa de Campo we can also find the Amusement Park and the Zoo-Aquarium of Madrid, together with the well-known Lago (lake) where you can practice rowing or go sailing. As we return by cableway to

❶ Teleférico
❷ Casa de Campo
❸ Templo de Debod
❹ Museo Cerralbo
❺ Plaza de España
❻ Jardines de Sabatini

15

Debod Temple

Casa de Campo Lake

the Paseo del Pintor Rosales, we will contemplate again the beautiful views of the Royal Palace and the Debod Temple, the next stop of our itinerary.

Templo de Debod

This little temple is located near the Paseo del Pintor Rosales, in front of Calle Ferraz.

The beginnings of its construction go back to the 4th century BC, the building is the original one brought from Egypt, and in its interior we can see the chapel dedicated to the gods Amon and Isis. The Egyptian State donated this faultless building to Spain in 1968 as a sign of gratitude for the help provided in salvaging the Abu Simbel temples, in Nubia. Since 1973, the temple can be visited and it is the only complete Egyptian temple (original construction)

that can be seen in our country. We should also underscore the place where the temple is situated for the beautiful views it offers, especially those of the Royal Palace and the Cathedral of La Almudena.

Leaving the Temple of Debod and contemplating in front of us the Tower of Madrid, we will head towards the Cerralbo Museum.

Museo Cerralbo

This beautiful house-museum can be found in the number seventeen of Calle de Ventura Rodríguez. From the street, we can see the old bay window and the garden embellished with little statues. As opposed to other buildings of historical interest, there is still nothing to announce us the great beauty that this house-museum encloses. Already at the hallway,

Debod Temple

19

Cerralbo Museum

Next page:
Plaza de España and Tower of Madrid

the **Staircase of Honour** takes us back to another epoch. This room is not only a passage to other areas but a space that, given its great beauty, should be admired with time, enjoying its magnificent decoration. In its walls we can see big tapestries and paintings from the 17th century, as well as the coat of arms of the Marquis of Cerralbo.

From here onwards, we will see a great collection of pieces of art and antique objects that the Marquises of Cerralbo gathered during their numerous journeys. One of the first rooms we will see in this visit is the **Religious Gallery**, from which we would like to underscore the painting (oil on canvass) *San Francisco en Éxtasis*, by El Greco. Afterward, we reach the **Painting Gallery**, where paintings by Alonso Cano, Zurbarán and Ribera, among others, are hung. Mounting the **Staircase of Honor**, we enter the **Armoury**, where we can see an exhibition of arms and medieval suits of armour. At the end of the corridor, we find the **Oriental Room**, where there is an exhibition of war objects belonging to Japan, The Philippines, and Morocco. The second floor, without doubt, also offers beautiful rooms such as the **State Dinning Room**, with a long table disposed for twenty-four guests and luxuriously equipped. In this room, important personalities met: politicians, writers, etc. The living room is decorated with paintings from the 17th to the 19th centuries. Other important rooms in this floor are the Study and the **Library**.

The **Library** stores thousands of volumes in a variety of subject matters. We can also see here some collections of antique objects: guns, pens, seals, etc. We finish our visit to the Cerralbo Museum in the **Ball Room**, decorated in marble with Venetian

I. From Paseo del Pintor Rosales to Calle de Bailén

mirrors and frescoes. All this exposed above makes the visit to this little-known museum worthwhile.

Plaza de España

This is one of the most important squares of the capital, where the Gran Vía ends, and Calle de la Princesa begins. In this last street, the Tower of Madrid, built by brothers Joaquín and Julián Otamendi in 1957, is located. This building was one of the first skyscrapers of the city. It was built over a lot situated in the corner of Calle de la Princesa facing Plaza de España and it was equipped with the fastest lifts at the time. In the central part of the square and in the direction of Calle Bailén, we can see landscaped areas and a monument to the work of Cervantes, with the statues of Don Quixote and Sancho Panza.

Jardines de Sabatini

These peaceful gardens offer us a good view of the north façade of the Royal Palace. The gardens were built over the old stables of Charles III and they owe their name to the architect Sabatini, also the architect of the Royal Palace. These gardens, together with those of Campo del Moro, surround the Royal Palace.

Gardens of Sabatini

From Plaza de la Encarnación to Cuesta de la Vega

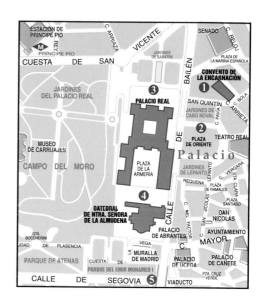

Convento de la Encarnación

Across from the Sabatini Gardens, following Calle de San Quintín, we reach the Plaza de la Encarnación, where an enclosed convent of the same name stands. It was built in 1616 by Juan Gómez de Mora and Friar Alberto de la Madre de Dios. The convent was very much connected to the Royal Palace and it keeps a great collection of paintings, most of them from the 17th century. We start our visit with a painting exhibition of great artistic value, even if many of the authors are unknown. The portraits of Philip III and Margaret of Austria, founders of the convent, are outstanding. We continue our visit through a corridor with large windows that lead to a central patio, where paintings of anonymous authors from the

Madrid of the time (17th century) are hung. At the end of the corridor, we enter an ample room where we can see the choir stalls next to the church and separated from it by a screen. Going down a set of stairs we enter one of the most curious rooms of the convent: **The Reliquary Museum**. Here, a big collection of crosses, boxes, coffers, etc. is being exhibited, the majority of them preserving in its interior little objects, human remains such as bones, skulls, or hair, and jewellery that belonged to different saints. The most important relic is an ampoule with the blood of Saint Pantaleón, whose special feature is that it liquefies every year in the day of the Saint, the 27th of June. We will finish our visit with the church (18th century), where we will contemplate again, to the left of the altar,

❶ *Convento de la Encarnación*
❷ *Plaza de Oriente*
❸ *Palacio Real*
❹ *Catedral de la Almudena*
❺ *Parque del Emir Mohamed I*

the screen that separates the church from the choir stalls.

Plaza de Oriente

Crossing Calle de San Quintín and passing through the Gardens of Cabo Noval, we reach Plaza de Oriente. The statue of Philip IV stands out in the centre of the square, a work by Pietro Tacca made in 1640. Galileo Galilei proposed to make the rear part of the statue solid and the front hollow, so that the horse could keep its balance over its two rear legs. Behind it we see the **Royal Palace**, and facing it is the **Royal Theatre**. Surrounded by gardens and big statues on its sides, this square invites you to relax. From here we can admire the wonderful façade of the Royal Palace, the highlight of this itinerary.

Palacio Real

This is the most important historical building of the capital and, next to The Prado Museum, the most visited. We have to go back to the 9th century when, in the same place that is occupied today by such beautiful building, stood the Alcázar, a fortress dedicated to the defence of these lands during the times of great battles. In the 16th century, Charles V and Philip II reconstructed it as Royal Palace but it would not be one until the 18th century when, after a big fire, Philip V built a new Royal Palace. The first thing we find in our visit is the big **Patio de Armas (Court of Arms)**, which soon invites us to proceed towards the first halls of the itinerary.

La Real Farmacia

Our first steps take us to the Royal Pharmacy, in which it is preserved and exhibited an important *botamen* (or set of jars belonging to a pharmacy) of the 18th century. In the following rooms we can see splendid ceramic and glass jars (18th-19th centuries), some coming from other royal pharmacies. Passing the first and second rooms of Charles IV, we reach, through a corridor, the **Distillation Hall**. The room is very interesting and its contents get our attention. In it we can see a reproduction of an alchemy laboratory of the 16th century. We see copper pieces used to distil medicinal substances, bronze mortars decorated with the coat of arms of Philip IV, a press to extract juices, glass vessels, etc. The **Royal Pharmacy** was founded by Philip II in 1594. To continue our itinerary we must step outside again to the **Court of Arms**.

Gardens of Plaza de Oriente

Statue of Philip IV in Plaza de Oriente

Calle Bailén and Royal Palace

▲

Court of Arms of the Royal Palace

Los Salones Reales (The Royal Chambers)
The main staircase, a beautiful marble work by Sabatini, leads us to the first lounges. After passing the **Salón de Alabarderos** and the **Salón de Columnas** we reach one of the most remarkable chambers of the palace, the **Salón del Trono** (The Throne Room). The decoration, Italian style for the most part, is exquisite. It combines the colours red (of the walls lined with velvet) and gold (of the furniture). The two throne chairs are decorated with golden lions and in the ceiling there is a magnificent painting in fresco. The rest of the room is filled with mirrors with golden embellishments and, in the centre, big lamps hung. Next we will find the **Saleta**, the **Antecámara** (antechamber), the **Cámara** (chamber) and the **Dormitorio de Carlos III** (the sleeping room of Charles III). In the antechamber, we can see paintings by Francisco de Goya. The sleeping room is the very chamber where Charles III died in 1788.

After visiting the Porcelain Room, **Sala de las Porcelanas**, all of it covered with porcelain tiles of Rococo style, and the **Saleta amarilla** (old study of Charles III), we reach another of the most significant rooms of the Royal Palace.

El Comedor de Gala (The State Dining Room)

The room surprises us with its extraordinary beauty and the good taste of its decoration. In the centre we see a long table that sits a hundred guests. An important part of the room (and its decoration) is of French style. In it we can see Chinese (18th century) and French (19th century) vases, wonderful paintings in fresco (in the ceiling) and many golden embellishments. Big tapestries of the 16th century complete the decoration, together with marble columns and beautiful lamps. Being in this room, it is easy to imagine how the celebrations and the balls at that time must have been, with the royalty and the nobility dressed for the occasion with period suits and dresses and assisted constantly by butlers, servants and musicians. We finish our visit to the Royal Palace seeing other rooms of interest, among which we wish to highlight the Music Hall **(Sala de Música)**, and the Royal Chapel **(la Real Capilla)**.

Catedral de la Almudena

Right outside the Royal Palace we find this graceful Cathedral. The works began in the

Cathedral of La Almudena.

year 1883 and His Holiness the Pope John Paul II consecrated it with the name Santa Iglesia Catedral de Nuestra Señora de la Almudena the 15th of June, 1993. Its initial architect was the Marquis of Cubas, who designed a Gothic cathedral. The construction of the actual cathedral was finished by Fernando Chueca and Carlos Sidro, in Neoclassical style, more in tune with the Royal Palace. Surrounding the cathedral we find the **Parque del Emir Mohamed I**, where we can see the remains of the antique Arab wall from the 9th century. In front of it can be found the access to the **Cript** of the Almudena Cathedral, which has a wonderful doorway worthy of admiration.

Sunset at the Cathedral of La Almudena.

Cathedral of La Almudena

From Plaza de San Andrés to Calle de Segovia

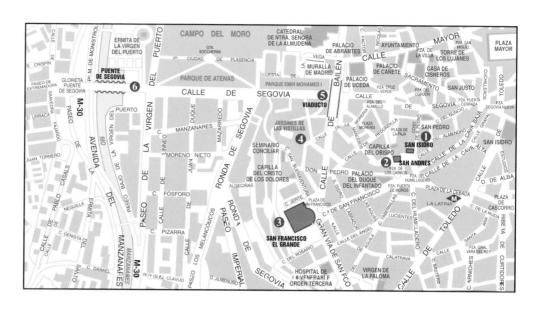

❶ *Museo de San Isidro*
❷ *Iglesia de San Andrés*
❸ *Basílica de San Francisco el Grande*
❹ *Las Vistillas*
❺ *Viaducto*
❻ *Puente de Segovia*

Museo de San Isidro

Passing by the Plaza de Puerta de Moros we reach the Plaza de San Andrés, where this little museum is found. Inside the museum, there are paintings, sculptures and drawings connected with the Patron Saint of Madrid, San Isidro Labrador, and the pre-history and medieval history of the city. The chapel dedicated to the saint (18th century) deserves special attention. It is placed where San Isidro died, inside we can see the **Pozo del Milagro**, the Miracle Well, in which San Isidro made the water rise thus saving his son from drowning, as well as the central patio, which is of Renaissance style.

Patio of the Museum of San Isidro

31

Iglesia de San Andrés y Capilla de San Isidro

Next to the Museum of San Isidro, we find this impeccable church with an impressive façade, high dome and doorway (18th century). As we enter the temple, our attention is caught by the altar, decorated with big columns to both sides and golden embellishments. The stained glass windows of the dome make a harmonious set with the rest of the decorative elements of the altar. Stepping outside again to the Plaza de Puerta de Moros, and turning to the right, we will be able to see in the background the next point of interest in our itinerary.

Basílica de San Francisco el Grande

This big building (one of the capital's best temples) keeps in its interior great works of historical and artistic interest. It was built in 1784 by Francisco Sabatini and Friar Francisco de las Cabezas. Big wooden doors lead us inside the building, which is of extraordinary beauty. The whole church is surrounded by chapels, each of them containing paintings in fresco of great artistic value. They are all interesting but we wish to highlight the **Capilla de San Bernardino**, which contains paintings by Francisco de Goya, including his self-portrait. The central dome is completely covered by big paintings in fresco dating from the 19th century. In the far end, at the altar, we can appreciate the 16th century walnut choir stalls.
But this is not the end of it, since the temple has other areas of great interest, which we shall see next.

The Museum

We start with the art gallery next to the altar. As we go in we see big paintings (17th-18th centuries) in the walls of two long corridors. By the walls we find many choir stalls belonging to the Franciscan monks of the congregation. Before finishing the visit through these corridors, we enter the **Antesacristía** (the antevestry). Again in this room we can see the choir stalls built in walnut and oak. The room is decorated with mirrors and paintings in fresco in the ceiling. Next, we entry the **Sacristía** (the vestry), where we can see 17th century paintings and paintings in fresco at both sides of the room. After visiting the vestry, we take the corridor again where we will find exposed some of the best oil paintings of the museum, belonging to painters such as Alonso Cano, Francisco de Zurbarán or Francisco Pacheco, among others.

Real Basílica de San Francisco El Grande

33

Calle Bailén Viaduct

Bridge of Segovia

Calle Bailén Viaduct

36

To finish our route we propose an agreeable walk that will take us through **Las Vistillas**, the **Viaducto** and the **Puente de Segovia**.

Leaving San Francisco el Grande and nearly without noticing, we reach the park of **Las Vistillas**. From here we can see beautiful pictures of the Almudena Cathedral and wonderful sunsets. Heading towards the **Puente de Segovia**, we can continue watching good panoramic views, especially when reaching Calle Bailén and the **Viaducto**. Due to tragic events, this bridge has been increased in height with reinforced glass. A bit later, we will reach the Athens Park –descending some stairs and passing underneath the bridge–, which is located in Calle Segovia, and from where we can enjoy a different perspective of the bridge. At the end of the street, we find the **Puente de Segovia**, the oldest bridge of Madrid, dating from 1584 and built by Juan de Herrera.

From Paseo de la Virgen del Puerto to Paseo de la Florida

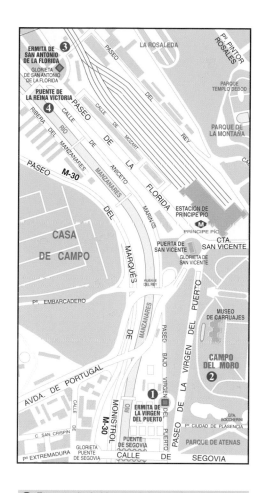

❶ *Ermita de la Virgen del Puerto*
❷ *Jardines del Campo del Moro*
❸ *Ermita de San Antonio de la Florida*
❹ *Puente de la Reina Victoria*

Ermita de la Virgen del Puerto

Next to the **Puente de Segovia**, we will find this little hermitage (Baroque style, 17th-18th century) built by Pedro de Ribera in 1718. It is located in a peaceful place and in its surroundings we can see landscaped areas and sport zones that invite the visitor to rest and relax.

After a nice walk around the hermitage, we will place ourselves in the Paseo de la Virgen del Puerto in the direction of the **Estación del Norte** in order to visit the gardens of Campo del Moro.

Jardines del Campo del Moro

In the very Paseo de la Virgen del Puerto we find a small door to the gardens and, after traversing a narrow path flanked by big trees, we reach the main avenue. The view is spectacular: at the far end of the landscaped street we see the Royal Palace, but here the building is not the most prominent feature of this beautiful picture. The rosebushes, the lawn, which seems a large green carpet, the central fountains, the ducks, the peacocks, and other birds, create an overall impression worth of being framed. The name of these

4. *From Paseo de la Virgen del Puerto to Paseo de la Florida*

Gardens of Campo del Moro

Gardens of Campo del Moro

gardens, Campo del Moro (Field of the Moor), comes from the time when Alí Ben Yusuf and his troops tried to reconquer Madrid and the Alcázar from Christian domination in the year 1109. Projects to create these gardens began after the fire that took place on the night of Christmas Eve in 1734 (together with the construction of the new Royal Palace), but its definite realisation did not take place until after the War of Independence. In these gardens we also find the Museum of Carriages (**Museo de Carruajes**).

After visiting the gardens of Campo del Moro, we continue straight taking the Paseo de la Virgen del Puerto, in the direction of Estación del Norte, turning left on the Paseo de la Florida, where we will visit a small museum of the brilliant painter Francisco de Goya.

Ermita de San Antonio de la Florida

The passage that leads us inside this small temple (constructed by Francisco Fontana in 1798) quickly places us in the hall of the museum. To the left, at the altar, we can see an ivory figure of Christ made in the 18th century and, to your feet, the sepulchre, where lie the mortal remains of the painter Francisco de Goya. However, more worthy of mention are the paintings in fresco that decorate the dome. Goya made here one of his best works, *Representación del milagro de San Antonio,* in which the saint resuscitates an assassinated man. The expressiveness of the characters' gestures, as well as the tones and colours used, are remarkable. In each corner of the room, there are mirrors tilted toward the ceiling so that

Hermitage of Virgen del Puerto

Hermitage of San Antonio de la Florida

41

Bridge of Reina Victoria

one can see the details of the paintings in fresco more comfortably.

We finish the route in front of the hermitage of San Antonio de la Florida, where we find the **Puente de la Reina Victoria**, a bridge built in 1909 by Eugenio Rivera. From here we will enjoy excellent views in a tranquil entourage close to the river Manzanares. On one side of the bridge, we see the cableway and, on the other, we make out the Cathedral of la Almudena.

42

From Calle de la Princesa to Calle de Toledo

Palacio de Liria

Palacio de Liria

Placing ourselves in Calle de la Princesa, in front of the tube station entrance of Ventura Rodríguez, we can see the **Palacio de Liria**, owned by the Dukes of Alba. The building is the work of Ventura Rodríguez

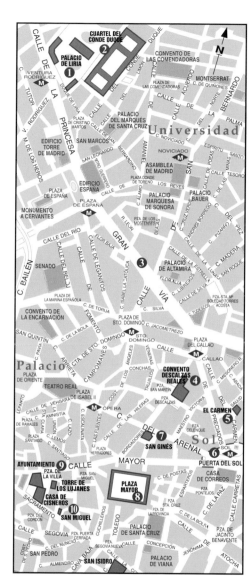

❶ *Palacio de Liria*
❷ *Cuartel del Conde Duque*
❸ *Gran Vía*
❹ *Convento de las Descalzas Reales*
❺ *Iglesia del Carmen*
❻ *Puerta del Sol*
❼ *Iglesia de San Ginés*
❽ *Plaza Mayor*
❾ *Plaza de la Villa. Ayuntamiento*
❿ *Iglesia de San Miguel*
⓫ *Iglesia de San Isidro*
⓬ *El Rastro*
⓭ *Puente de Toledo*

Plaza de España and Gran Vía

Headquarters of Conde Duque

and Francisco Sabatini, and it was built in 1783. It keeps works of art of great artistic value. One day a week, groups are allowed to visit some of the palace rooms, by appointment.

We proceed along Calle del Duque de Liria to take Calle de Las Negras right away in the direction of Calle del Conde Duque.

Cuartel del Conde Duque

The first thing that catches our attention of these headquarters, apart from their rectangular façade, is the main door decorated with a large shield, all built by Pedro de Ribera in 1754. The building was one of the biggest of its time, and in its interior we can find the Town Newspaper Archive (la **Hemeroteca Municipal**), the Town Historical Library (la **Biblioteca Histórica Municipal**) and the Musical Library of Madrid (la **Biblioteca Musical de Madrid**). We can also see periodic exhibitions on diverse matters.

Convent of Las Descalzas Reales

On the way to our next stop, we will pass by Plaza de España, to go up **Gran Vía** until we reach Plaza de Callao. Once we are in this square, we will go down the commercial street of Preciados to step, a few minutes later, in the Plaza de Las Descalzas, that we access through Calle Maestro Victoria.

Convento de las Descalzas Reales

Before being a convent it was a palace belonging to Charles I, and in it the Empress Mary of Austria was born in 1536. In 1559, it was transformed into a convent, where the Empress Mary, daughter of Charles the I and widow of Maximilian II of Germany, shut herself away.

In this enclosed convent we will also see (as we did in the convent of *la Encarnación*) big works of art, many of them by anonymous authors.

The first area of the convent that strikes our attention is the staircase that leads to the upper floors, there we see large paintings in

fresco from the middle of the 17th century. Going up to the first floor –by the extremely antique staircase whose walls and ceiling are decorated with magnificent Baroque frescoes– we reach a corridor that surrounds the central patio of the building, where one can see several chapels with wooden statues painted in oils from the 16th and 17th centuries: *Cristo Yacente* (Reclining Christ), *San José* (Saint Joseph), etc. There are some wooden doors (16th century) that remain from the times when it was a palace, one of them leads us to the following room where we can see three new chapels. Going up some stairs, we enter one of the most important chambers, a room containing the choir stalls and the remains of the Empress Mary of Austria. On one side of the sepulchre, we can admire a carving of *La Dolorosa,* by Pedro de Mena (17th century). After passing by the chapel dedicated to the Virgin of Guadalupe, we ascend to the third floor where we can contemplate large tapestries (18th century) made in wool and silk. Here is where the antique common dormitory of the convent nuns was placed.

Going down the main staircase, we will visit the rest of the rooms, where we can see portraits of the Royal family at the time, among other paintings. In these last rooms, we can admire important painters such as: Del Bosco, Luca Giordano, Zurbarán, Rubens and Murillo.

Stepping outside the Plaza de las Descalzas, we will cross Calle Preciados in order to see the ancient church **Iglesia del Carmen**, after which we will go down Calle del Carmen until we reach Puerta del Sol.

Puerta del Sol

Or Kilometer Zero, as it is also known this famous square of Madrid. This is the place

Equestrian statue of Charles III in Puerta del Sol

Previous page: Puerta del Sol

where the turn of year is celebrated traditionally, with the strokes of the Puerta del Sol clock. The most outstanding building is the **Casa de Correos** (the old Post), the actual central office of the Community of Madrid, built in 1768 by Jaime Marquet. The clock was installed in 1866. After visiting the Puerta del Sol, we will take Calle Arenal to see the **Iglesia de San Ginés**, which dates from 1672, even though later reforms make this fact unrecognizable.

We will continue taking the passage of San Ginés, as we head towards the most important square of the capital.

La Plaza Mayor

Crossing Calle Mayor, we enter the most beautiful and visited square of the city. The first Plaza Mayor was built in the 17th century, but after suffering several fires, it was reconstructed in its actual form by Juan de Villanueva in the 19th century. It is a meeting point for different cultural and popular events, and every Sunday the square arcades are transformed into a big market dedi-

Church of San Ginés

Plaza Mayor

Plaza Mayor

Plaza Mayor

cated to the selling and buying of antique stamps and coins. In the centre of the square, it is set the slender statue of Philip III riding a horse, the work of Juan de Bolonia. The square arcades give shelter to numerous bars and shops. It is a popular custom to taste the squid sandwiches, the *tapas* and wines offered in the *mesones* or inns that also surround the square. According to another tradition, the Plaza Mayor will also transform itself during Christmas time into a stage for many celebrations, and a market of itinerant stands, which sell figures to adorn the typical Christmas trees and nativity scenes.

Plaza de la Villa

There are several buildings in this square, among which we will visit the Town Hall or Ayuntamiento, built by Juan Gómez de Mora in 1695. Even though this building is commonly visited by people registered in Madrid to solve problems related with the Town Hall, there are also rooms that are visited because of their artistic and historical interest. We will start the visit admiring several paintings of personalities connected with the Town Hall, marquises and counts of the 19th century for the most part, all of them prior mayors of Madrid. At the end of a corridor, we access several rooms decorated with period furniture, where we can see large canvasses and objects of great historical value, such as some parchments (titles) dated between the 13th and 14th centuries, and that are exposed in glass showcases. We finish our visit in the ancient **Salón de Plenos** (Plenary Session Hall), this beautiful lounge leads to another spacious hall beautifully decorated known as **Patio de los Cristales** (Glass Patio). This room is surrounded by little sculptures of illustrious characters, such as Quevedo, Claudio Coello, Lope de Vega, etc. A beautiful polychromatic stained glass window in the ceiling completes the decoration of this room.

In front of the Town Hall door, taking the narrow Calle del Codo, we reach Calle Puñonrostro, where we will see the Church of San Miguel. The height of the temple is striking as well as its interior with numerous chapels. The church was built by Santiago Bonavia in 1745. After visiting the **Church of San Miguel**, we will head toward another of the most relevant temples of the capital.

Colegiata de San Isidro

This big building (17th-18th centuries), which shelters the remains of the Patron Saint Isidro Labrador, is situated in the popular district of La Latina (in Calle Toledo). Its interior is of great beauty, with many chapels dedicated to different saints like, for example, San Isidro and Santa María de la Cabeza.

Calle de Toledo and Colegiata de San Isidro

El Rastro. Calle de Ribera de Curtidores

El Rastro

To fully enjoy this visit we will have to undertake this itinerary on a Sunday or on a holiday. It is in those days when you can really breath the popular atmosphere of this itinerant market. Nowadays, the bazaar already starts in the Plaza de la Cebada, even if it is in the Plaza de Cascorro and in Calle de Ribera de Curtidores where one can find the biggest concentration of stands of every kind. In the aforementioned street you can also find antique stores. The number of people concentrated in these streets of Madrid is so large that, at midmorning, you can hardly walk, especially along Ribera de Curtidores.

The market offers a great variety of products, one can buy clothes and complements, decoration objects and antiques, coloured prints, comics, birds...everything is possible at El Rastro. In its surroundings, there are many bars, perfect to have an appetizer, or sample different dishes as traditional as the *cocido madrileño* (a typical stew made of chickpeas, bacon, meat, vegetables, etc.).

We will finish our route strolling until we reach the popular **Puente de Toledo**, of robust architecture, with little shrines dedicated to the Patron Saints of Madrid. The bridge of Toledo was built by Pedro de Ribera in 1732. The shrines are the work of Juan Alonso Villabrille and Ron.

Bridge of Toledo

From Calle de O'Donnell to Paseo de Recoletos

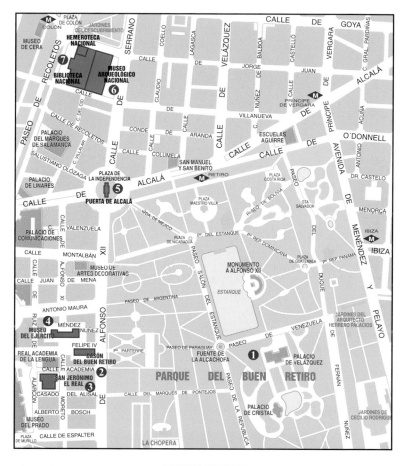

Parque del Buen Retiro

The Retiro Park (17th century) was used by the royalty as a place of amusement, for the organization of numerous parties. El Real Sitio del Buen Retiro (The Royal Site of Good Retreat) was a present made by the Count-Duke of Olivares to the King Philip IV. The name of *Retiro* or retreat is owed to the fact that this is the place where the kings of the time retired during periods of mourning and during Lent. In 1868, these grounds became the Town Hall property and their doors were opened to the public. From then onwards, el Parque del Buen Retiro has been one of the favourite places for the people of Madrid. With the passing of time, different modifications have been made in the park, for example, until the sixties decade of the 20th century, the Zoo or **Casa de Fieras**, was located there. We start our itinerary throughout the park from the **Montaña Artificial** (artificial mountain), in front of the number nine of Calle O'Donnell, heading towards the **Jardines de Cecilio Rodríguez**. These gardens are decorated with beautiful iron arches. We go in through a central passage with fountains to both sides and columns surrounded by flowers, where we can also see wonderful

❶ *Parque del Buen Retiro*
❷ *Casón del Buen Retiro*
❸ *San Jerónimo El Real*
❹ *Museo del Ejército*
❺ *Plaza de la Independencia. Puerta de Alcalá*
❻ *Museo Arqueológico Nacional*
❼ *Biblioteca Nacional*

53

Pond of El Retiro Park

Glass Palace

Monument to Alfonso XII next to the pond of El Retiro Park

peacock specimens. After visiting the gardens of Cecilio Rodríguez, we continue our walk along El Retiro in the direction of **La Rosaleda** (the Rosegarden). As its name indicates, we can here admire a great variety of rosebushes in a space surrounded by trees and embellished with fountains. From the Rosegarden, we head ourselves to one of the most interesting areas of El Retiro.

El Palacio de Cristal

Considered one of the jewels of Spanish architecture in iron and glass, this building

was built in 1887 as a green house-pavilion for an exhibition of flowers and plants coming from The Philippines. The Glass Palace is set next to a small lake where turtles, ducks and swans glide past, forming a beautiful picture. In this building, one can see periodical exhibitions of different matters. Very close to the Glass Palace we can find the **Palacio de Velázquez** (1883), used in actuality as exhibition hall. The architect Ricardo Velázquez built both palaces for the 1887 Colonial Exhibition. After a little walk, we reach the most central and lively place of the park, the **Estanque del Retiro**, where you can go for a row. A long avenue borders the pond, in it one can enjoy different itinerant shows: puppet shows, musicians, clowns, fortune-tellers, etc. On the other side of the pond, stands the **Monumento a Alfonso XII**, an important landmark of this park, which was inaugurated in 1922. It is the work of several sculptors, Mariano

Glass Palace Lake

Benlliure among them. We leave the Parque del Buen Retiro by the door of Philip IV, admiring on our way the gardens of the **Paseo del Parterre** (the Flowerbed Walk), one of the oldest of the park.

Casón del Buen Retiro

Facing the door of Philip IV we find this ancient theatre and ballroom, where the plays of Calderón de la Barca or Lope de Vega were performed. Nowadays, it is part of **The Prado Museum**. It was built in 1656 as part of the now lost Palace of the Good Retreat (Palacio del Buen Retiro).
Very close to El Casón del Buen Retiro we find the **Iglesia de San Jerónimo El Real** (gothic style, 16th-17th centuries) and the **Museo del Ejército** (Army Museum), where one can admire the spade Tizona of El Cid Campeador, don Rodrigo Díaz de Vivar (1043-1099). The visit around this museum allows us to get to know halls of great interest, such as the **Salón de Reinos**, where one can find a small Arab Room (**Sala Árabe**) decorated like the Alhambra of Granada. Also deserve attention the **Sala de la Guerra de la Independencia** and the **Hall of Carlos I**, where one can see an Indo-Portuguese tent of the 16th century. This museum exposes a great variety of antique weapons; one can see cannons, guns, rifles, etc., as well as uniforms, flags, and decorations.
As we exit the Army Museum, we place ourselves again in the Casón del Buen Retiro and, facing the outside of The Retiro Park, we will go up Calle de Alfonso XII

Church of San Jerónimo El Real

until we reach the **Plaza de la Independencia**, where **Puerta de Alcalá** is set. It was built in 1778 during the reign of Charles III, after a project presented by Sabatini. This monumental door emits beauty day and night, and it is a symbol of Madrid. The square is crossed by three big streets, one of them is Calle Serrano, which we will take in order to make our next visit.

Museo Arqeológico

A few steps away Independence Square, one finds this great museum. We recommend

Puerta de Alcalá

59

Entry to the Archaeological Museum

starting the itinerary with the prehistoric halls, las **Salas de la Prehistoria**, in which the fossilized remains of different "hominids" are exposed, and we are explained how those first steps in human evolution took place. In some of the following rooms, we can see the remains found in different archaeological sites, such as the one in Atapuerca (Burgos), San Isidro (Madrid) or the elephant remains found in Torralba and Ambrona (Soria). Continuing the visit along the **Salas de la Edad de Bronce** (Bronze Age Gallery) and those rooms dedicated to the Iron Age, la **Edad de Hierro**, we will visit the halls dedicated to the prehistory of the Balearic and Canary Islands, **Salas dedicadas a la Prehistoria de las Islas Baleares y Canarias**. We will proceed through the room dedicated to Ancient Egypt, **Sala del Antiguo Egipto y Nubia**. Here the exhibition of mommies and Egyptian sarcophaguses deserve special attention, as well as the collection of amulets and beetles. We continue our route through this interesting building in the upper floor, one of the most attractive floors of this museum. The first thing that catches our attention is the high funerary tower of Pozo Moro (a reconstruction of the remains found in Albacete), next we can see the Lady of Baza and the Lady of Elche, two of the main jewels of this museum. These first rooms lead us to others dedicated to Roman Spain, **Salas dedicadas a la Hispania Romana**. Strolling along the long corridors of the exhibition we can see large mosaics (3rd and 2nd centuries BC) found in Zaragoza, Albacete, Valencia or Palencia, or the wonderful Roman tables of Bronze (Flavian period, 1st century) coming from Sevilla. In those tables, an important part of the law that regulated town life in this Roman city is collected. It is also important to mention the room in which the treasure of Guarrazar, dis-

Archaeological Museum

National Library

covered near Toledo, is exposed. This ancient and valuable medieval treasure is composed of different jewels, many of them are made of gold, and some are decorated with precious stones and pearls, such as the crowns and crosses.

We can continue with our route going up the following floors, to which we will have access by a wonderful marble staircase decorated with columns and sculptures. Here we will see the periodical exhibitions of the museum: paintings, sculptures, drawings, etc., or the Noble Halls, where organ concerts are offered with the only *Órgano Realejo* that can be found in Madrid (this is a small manual organ dating from the 18th century). In the garden, to the left of the entry, we can see a reproduction of the **Altamira Caves** (Cantabria).

To finish the itinerary, we will visit the **Book Museum**, placed inside the **National Library**. We should underscore the manuscripts from the 15th and 16th centuries, especially the Books of Hours, considered true works of art.

From Plaza de Colón to Calle de Lope de Vega

❶ Jardines del Descubrimiento
❷ Centro Cultural de la Villa
❸ Fuente de la Cibeles
❹ Museo Thyssen-Bornemisza
❺ Fuente de Neptuno
❻ Congreso de los Diputados
❼ Iglesia de Jesús de Medinaceli
❽ Casa de Lope de Vega
❾ Convento de las Trinitarias Descalzas

Gardens of El Descubrimiento
in Plaza de Colón

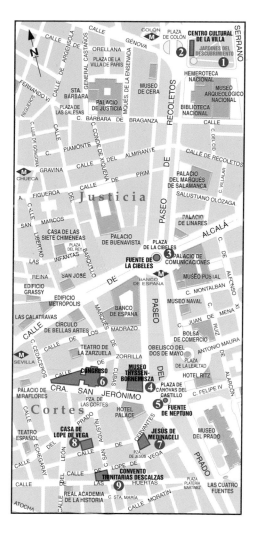

Plaza de Colón

This square owes its name to Christopher Columbus (discoverer of America), to whom the elevated monument that rises next to the **Centro Cultural de la Villa**, and which was inaugurated in 1892, pays homage. Below the square and adjoining the waterfall, lies this cultural centre in whose auditorium-theatre different cultural events are celebrated, and where one can see periodical exhi-

bitions about diverse matters. On the other side of the square (Calle Serrano), one finds the **Jardines del Descubrimiento** –built in 1977– where we shall begin this itinerary. After taking a stroll around Plaza de Colón (and after visiting, if we feel like it, the **Museo de Cera** (The Wax Museum), situated in front of Columbus Statue), we will go down Paseo de Recoletos for a few minutes until we reach the famous fountain of Cibeles.

Plaza de Colón

Cibeles Fountain

Plaza de Cibeles

This square is surrounded by four important buildings, one in each corner of the square, the **The Army Headquarters-Buenavista Palace**, the **Linares Palace**, the **Bank of Spain** and the **Palacio de Comunicaciones** (or Main Post). However, every glance converges in the Fountain of Goddess Cibeles, la **Fuente de Cibeles**, considered to be the most beautiful and popular of Madrid. It is placed in the centre of the square and it is visited and admired by thousands of tourists every year. The fountain was designed by Ventura Rodríguez and built in 1782.

Museo Thyssen-Bornemisza

This art gallery, the ancient Palace of Villahermosa (18th century), is located very close to Plaza de Cibeles (Paseo del Prado, n° 8). The building gathers in its interior a large number of works of art from a variety of styles and periods, such as the gothic paintings or the Cubism of the beginning of the 20th century. The museum was inaugurated the 8th of October, 1992 by the kings of Spain, don Juan Carlos and doña Sofía. Many are the people who visit this museum because of the quality of the works it gathers and its central location (very close to The Prado Museum). We start our itinerary admiring the religious works of Italian authors (tempera over panel), of the 16th century for the most part. After visiting the rooms dedicated to Italian and German painting (16th century), we reach a room with paintings of El Greco and Tintoretto, among others (oil on canvass), to continue with other oil painting by Rivera and Caravaggio. At the end of a corridor, we enter another hall that stands out because of a large painting (oil on canvass) of Luca Giordano, *Solomon Judgement.* In the following room, we continue seeing works of art of great artistic value, such as the canvass of *La Virgen y el Niño* by Murillo. But there are other oils over canvass worthy of attention, like the *Venus and Cupid* and *Portrait of a Young Lady* painted by Rubens.

In another of the Museum floors, we can see paintings of the 17th and 18th centuries, landscapes, still lives and portraits for the most part. When we reach the middle of the floor, we will be able to see paintings by Francisco de Goya. In the following room, we can proceed with our visit admiring the impressionist paintings, in particular the oil

Neptune Fountain 67

on canvass *Woman with parasol in a garden* of Renoir.

We finish our itinerary visiting the rooms that exhibit paintings (oils over panel, canvass and cardboard) by Picasso and Joan Miró, among others. There are many outstanding authors represented in this museum that have not been mentioned in this summary, but lastly we would like to underscore the surrealist paintings of Salvador Dalí, such as *Sueño causado por el vuelo de una abeja alrededor de una granada un segundo antes de despertar* (Dream caused by the flight of a bee over a pomegranate a second before waking up).

In the home straight of our itinerary, we will pass by the **Fuente de Neptuno** (designed by Ventura Rodríguez and built in 1782) and by the **Congreso de los Diputados** (1850) (House of Commons), to visit a little bit later the **Iglesia de Jesús de Medinaceli** (1922). Afterwards, we will go up until we reach the number 11 of Calle Cervantes and we visit the **Casa de Lope de Vega**. In this picturesque house lived, for the last twenty-five years of his life, the writer Lope de Vega. The house (17th century) preserves some goods and chattels, period furniture, and a chapel dedicated to the Patron Saint of Madrid San Isidro Labrador.

We finish our itinerary through Calle Lope de Vega, along which we will find the **Convento de las Trinitarias** (17th century) where Cervantes was buried.

House of Commons

From Calle de Santa Isabel to Plaza de Murillo

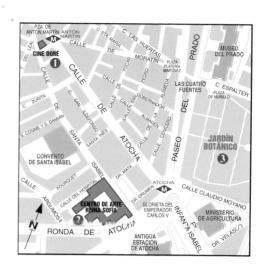

❶ Cine Doré
❷ Centro de Arte Reina Sofía
❸ Jardín Botánico

Cine Doré

Convent and Street of Santa Isabel

The itinerary begins in the old **Cine Doré**, the central office of the National Film Archive. Going down Calle Santa Isabel (and passing by the **Convento de Santa Isabel**) we reach the square where the **Centro de Arte Reina Sofía** is located.

Centro de Arte Reina Sofía

This big Art Centre was installed inside an old **General Hospital** built in 1781 and it now offers a large number of periodical and permanent exhibitions the whole year round. The external lifts create a contrast with the classical lines of the façade. The museum provides four floors for the different types of exhibitions, two floors for the periodical ones and the other two for the permanent ones.

Gardens of the Reina Sofía Art Centre

Reina Sofía Art Centre

Itinerary around some of the permanent exhibitions

After taking a stroll around the central gardens of the ground floor, the external lifts will transport us to the upper floors. We will start the visit with some paintings by Vasque and Catalonian artists. This room, dedicated to the **Origins of Modernity in Contemporary Spanish Art**, leads us to one of the most relevant rooms of this floor. After going through a corridor, where works by José Gutiérrez Solana, Juan Gris and Pablo Gargallo are exposed, we reach the **Sala de Pablo Picasso**. In this room, we will see some oils over canvass, paintings made with graphite and ink over paper, and sketches of the *Guernica*.

In the centre of a long room, we see a varnished bronze sculpture, and next to it a large oil on canvass (349 x 776 cm.), the *Guernica* (1937). Adjoining this room, we find another of the most outstanding halls, where the works of Joan Miró are exposed. Here we see pictures whose main characteristic lies in their apparent simplicity. Among Joan Miró's works, which are made with different materials, three big paintings made with acrylic paint over canvass stand out, as well as the oil on canvass titled *Mujer, pájaro y estrella* (Woman, Bird and Star). We will finish our walk through the **Sala de Joan Miró** to proceed to the hall of the brilliant painter **Salvador Dalí**. We will see some oils over cardboard and canvass to begin with, and then some oils over papier mâché and canvass, over which stands the painting *La muchacha en la ventana (Young woman at the window),* an excellent and very well known work by this Catalonian painter.

To finish this brief summary, we wish to highlight some of the rooms dedicated to the Spanish Art of the 20s and 30s, as well as those dedicated to Spanish sculpture, where one can also find sculptures by Joan Miró.

Leaving the Reina Sofía Art Centre, we will go down in the direction of **Atocha Train Station**, and we will turn to the left to take Paseo del Prado, which will lead us to Plaza de Murillo.

Real Jardín Botánico

This garden is located in the area of Madrid most visited by tourists, facing the Door of Murillo of **The Prado Museum**. This garden contains a great variety of trees and exotic plants brought from all over the world. In 1756, Ferdinand VI ordered the creation of

Plaza de Murillo

a Botanical Garden close to the Manzanares River. Twenty years later, Charles III gave the order to move it to its actual location, inaugurating it in the year 1781. Apart from the wonderful plant and tree collection that this botanical garden offers, one can also visit the green houses, such as the one for Exhibitions, inaugurated by the kings of Spain don Juan Carlos y doña Sofía the 12th of May 1993. This green house contains outstanding cactuses, some of enormous size, specially those coming from the American and African continent. Next we will visit **The Prado Museum**, which is very close to the Botanical Garden.

Royal Botanical Garden

From Paseo del Prado to Puerta del Sol

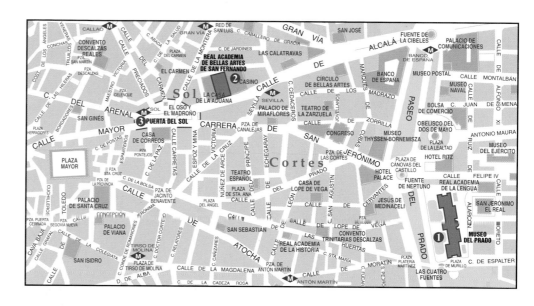

❶ Museo del Prado
❷ Real Academia de Bellas Artes de San Fernando
❸ Puerta del Sol

The Four Fountains

Paseo del Prado

This itinerary starts in Paseo del Prado, where some of the most important landmarks of the city such as **The Neptune Fountain**, the **Thyssen-Bornemisza Museum** or the **Botanical Garden**, already mentioned in other itineraries, are located. We recommend enjoying the walk in full, either starting from Plaza del Emperador Carlos V, or from Plaza de Cibeles.

Museo del Prado

The most important and visited museum of Madrid is situated midway along Paseo del Prado. It is acknowledged to be one of the best art galleries in the world. The construc-

75

El Prado Museum

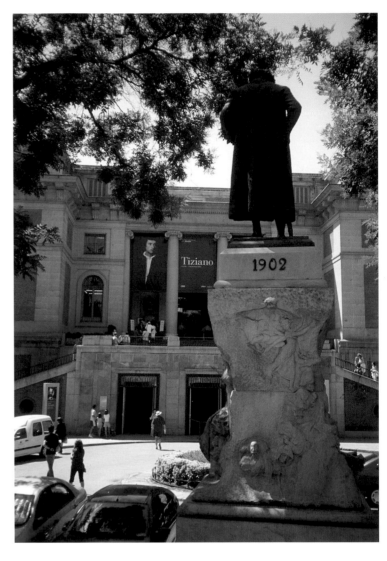

Paseo del Prado

El Prado Museum.
Door of Francisco de Goya

tion of the building is the work of Juan de Villanueva (18th century), who also participated, together with Sabatini, in the Botanical Garden project. The museum has three monumental doors: the Door of Murillo, which leads to the Botanical Garden, the Door of Velázquez, facing Paseo del Prado and Francisco de Goya Door, situated on the other wing of the building.

Itinerary through The Prado Museum

We enter the museum through the low door of Goya. Right at the entry we can see a corridor with large reredos with religious paintings (15th century). This corridor leads us to the ground floor where we will start seeing paintings of the 14th century, for the most part painted over panel, the most relevant of which are the works of the painter Rafael Sanzio. Further on we will be able to see Italian paintings from the 14ᵗʰ until the 16ᵗʰ centuries, and admire the works of Tintoretto, Basano and Veronés. Before finishing our visit to this floor, we would like to underscore the rooms dedicated to the Italian and Spanish Schools of the 16ᵗʰ century, where we can see paintings by artists as important as Tiziano or El Greco. In this hall, we can contemplate the portraits of knights of the period such as the famous oil *El caballero de la mano en el pecho* by El Greco. Before going up to the other floors we can go down the basement, where one will find the **Treasure of the Dolphin**. This treasure is composed of a great collection of decorative and table pieces (16ᵗʰ-18ᵗʰ centuries) carved, for the most part, out of rock crystal and adorned with precious stones and gold.

Upper Floors

We will continue our visit proceeding to the upper floors, where there are exposed sketches and templates of the tapestries made in the Royal Factory of Tapestry of Santa Barbara. These designs, which were to decorate the lounges and rooms of the palace, were commissioned to the painter Francisco de Goya. Among them, deserve special attention: *El albañil borracho (The Drunk Bricklayer)*, *La ermita de San Isidro en el día de la fiesta (San Isidro Hermitage during a Holiday)*, or *La gallinita ciega (Blind Man's Buff)*. In this floor, one can also see very famous works by Goya, such as *La maja vestida y La maja desnuda*.

The Itinerary's Home Straight

We will finish this summary of the most important halls visiting another of the essential floors. It is evident that Francisco de Goya is one of the painters better represented in

the museum, in terms of the quantity and quality of his works, and so we will continue admiring an ample exhibition dedicated to

El Prado Museum. Door of Murillo   79

this painter. We will start by **Salas de la Quinta del Sordo** (dark paintings), of which we should underscore the painting (mural painting into canvass) *Saturno devorando a uno de sus hijos (Saturn devouring one of his sons)*. This painting was painted in one of the lower floor façade walls of The Deaf Man Villa (Quinta del Sordo), a house where Goya lived and suffered an illness that left him deaf. We will continue seeing large oils painted by Goya, but we would not like to finish this chapter without highlighting the great oil on canvass, *Los fusilamientos del tres de mayo*. After admiring the rooms dedicated to Goya, we give way to other painters such as Murillo, by whom we can admire paintings, mainly of religious content, as famous as *La Inmaculada de El Escorial* or *Los niños de la concha,* among others. Passing by the rooms dedicated to Zurbarán, Alonso Cano and Claudio Coello, we reach the great **Sala de Velázquez**, where we can contemplate and admire the master piece of *Las Meninas (The Maids of Honour)*. Much has been written about this key work by Velázquez, but this is not the only important work of this author that is being exhibited in The Prado Museum. There are also outstanding pieces such as *Las Hilanderas* or the great canvass of *Las Lanzas o la Rendición de Breda*. We will finish our visit around The Prado Museum, enjoying some Flemish and Dutch paintings of the 17th century. The most important rooms are those dedicated to the painter Rubens. Among his paintings, we would like to highlight the oils *Adoration of the Magi,* where we can see that the painter has included himself in the scene by doing his self-portrait, and *The Three Graces,* the naked portrait of three women, one of whom was the second wife of the painter. To continue with our itinerary we will go up Calle de Alcalá (in the direction of

Puerta del Sol) and we will visit another of the most important art galleries of Madrid.

Real Academia de Bellas Artes de San Fernando

The Royal Academy was inaugurated by Ferdinand VI in he year 1752, but it was not until 1773 that it was moved to the actual building it now occupies, located at number thirteen of Calle de Alcalá. In 2002, the Museum had thirty-five rooms, and today it already has fifty-seven rooms open to the public. This enlargement coincided with the 250 anniversary of the Royal Academy, when the kings of Spain don Juan Carlos and doña Sofía came to inaugurate the exhibition "Ferdinand VI and Barbara of Braganza", in homage to the founder of the *Real Academia de Bellas Artes de San Fernando*. Outside this museum, it is not common to see large cues, as in other museums of the same category, however, the works exposed in this museum are of a very high level.

To visit the art gallery, we will have to go up by a staircase decorated with columns to the first floor, where we will start seeing oils by Francisco Pacheco, Zurbarán and El Greco. Next, a small room offers us two options: to the right, **Salas de Ribera and Alonso Cano**, and to the left, **Salas de Murillo, Rubens and Goya**. Entering the rooms to the left, we will see wonderful oils by Murillo: *Éxtasis de San Francisco de Asís, La Magdalena*. Continuing with our visit, we reach a room where the famous painting by Rubens *Susana and The Old Men* (or *La casta Susana*) is exhibited. Another painting that catches our attention is *The Spring* (16th century oil on panel) painted by Giuseppe Arcimboldo, the only painting by

this author that is exposed in Spain. In the painting we can see an original composition of a person's side portrait formed by a *collage* of numerous flowers. In the following rooms, we can contemplate a great collection of oils by the painter Francisco de Goya, among which are little paintings such as *Toros en un pueblo, Procesión con penitentes* and *Entierro de la sardina*. It remains to be said that this is only a brief account of everything one can see here. The museum also offers permanent sculpture exhibitions and different periodical exhibitions throughout the year.

After visiting the Royal Academy of Fine Arts of San Fernando, we will reach **Puerta del Sol**, where we will finish the *Itineraries around the city of Madrid* in order to give way to the routes and trips to the important towns of Madrid. We will finish our itineraries with a trip to Toledo.

Statue of "El Oso y el Madroño" in Puerta del Sol

Kilometre 0 in Puerta del Sol

81

Routes and Trips around the Community of Madrid

10

From Buitrago del Lozoya to Cotos

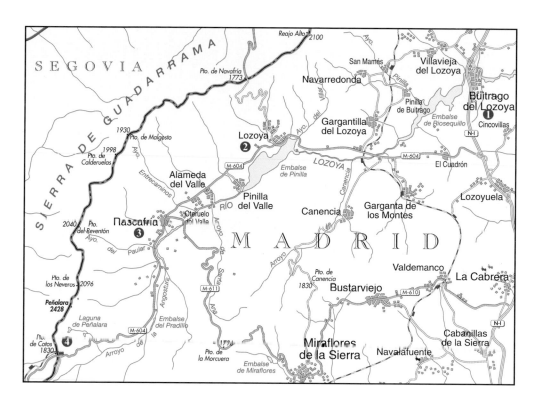

We will start this section of *Routes and Trips around the Community of Madrid* with the most outstanding area of Madrid's Northern Sierra.

Buitrago del Lozoya

Taking the N-I, and not many kilometres away from Madrid (74 km), we find the town of Buitrago, which surprises us with its great walled enclosure. Walking along its streets will take us to Plaza de Picasso, where we will start our itinerary around this medieval town.

Museo Picasso. "Colección Eugenio Arias"

The Town Hall is located in Plaza de Picasso. Inside the Town Hall we find this little museum which offers an ample collection of drawings, books and ceramic that Picasso gave to his intimate friend and barber Eugenio Arias, born in Buitrago del Lozoya. The collection reflects the great friendship shared by Picasso and Eugenio Arias, as we can see in the dedications that accompany the works exposed. The first things that we see in our visit throughout the museum are books and drawings, followed by clay objects decorated, for the most part, with bullfighting scenes. We can also see barber tools such as those contained in a wooden box pyroengraved by Picasso. We will finish the visit watching posters, more books, stamps and photographs of the time.

❶ *Buitrago del Lozoya*
❷ *Lozoya*
❸ *Rascafría*
❹ *Cotos*

Alcázar de Buitrago del Lozoya

Walk along the walled enclosure

This walled enclosure is the best of the Community of Madrid, due to its beautiful location and the fact that is flanked by the Lozoya River. As we go in by Calle del Arco, we will see the ancient clock tower. This passage will lead us to the church of Santa María del Castillo (14th-15th centuries) placed in a small square called Plaza de los

Caídos, with its high tower and a beautiful little entry that leads to the temple. To one side of the church there are some stairs that reach the top of the wall (13th-14th centuries). Walking along the wall we can reach one of its ends, and contemplate from there the river as it encircles the town of Buitrago. We can also walk along the other side of the wall, where the remains of the castle or *alcázar* (14th-15th centuries) are found. From there one can also contemplate a nice view of the beautiful setting formed by the Lozoya River and the walls with its seven towers surrounding the circular *plaza*.

We leave Buitrago del Lozoya heading toward Madrid and, after six kilometres, we take the exit to Rascafría. After driving for fourteen kilometres, we reach the Pinilla reservoir.

Buitrago del Lozoya

87

Puente del Perdón and Monastery of El Paular

Pinilla Reservoir

Lozoya

Little after spotting the reservoir, we reach this town famous for its natural entourage. Inside the town, it is worth seeing the Church of San Salvador (16th century).

We continue our route heading toward Rascafría without missing the beautiful scenery offered by the Pinilla reservoir. Before reaching the town of Rascafría, we will pass by the towns: Pinilla del Valle, Alameda del Valle, and Oteruelo del Valle.

Rascafría

We now visit one of the most outstanding towns of this route, especially because of its natural surroundings. Leaving the town, we

will head ourselves toward the Monastery of El Paular. The road that leads to the Monastery (2 km) is lined with great trees, beautiful meadows and numerous streams.

The Bridge and the Monastery

After enjoying a nice ride, we meet the **Puente del Perdón** (18th century) and the **Monasterio de El Paular** (14th-15th centu-ries), the first Carthusian convent set in Castilla. It is said that the Puente del Perdón (Forgiveness Bridge) owes its name to the belief that it was there where the culprits were judged. To one side of the bridge (next to the river) there are some houses built in wood that offer tourist information about the area and organise many guided hikes. Facing the bridge, we find the monastery.

▲

Monastery of El Paular

◀

Puente del Perdón

91

Landscape of Rascafría

Las Presillas

Monasterio de El Paular

A long passage leads us to a colonnaded patio and, at the end of the patio, a little door invites us to enter the monastery. The first thing we see is a big vestibule decorated with large shields in the ceiling and walls. On the right hand side of the entry door, we discover a great gothic door (15th century).

After a few minutes walk, we enter the great cloister. The landscaped central patio is surrounded by corridors, where the cells, in which the Carthusian monks lived, are situated. It especially catches our attention the little windows we find next to each cell through which the monks received their food. Leaving these corridors, we can admire the landscaped patio, which is predominantly of gothic style. We continue the visit through some internal corridors that lead us to the church, where we can appreciate

a lovely altar piece, baroque style, which occupies the frontal part of the altar and which surprises the visitor with its large dimensions. After the altar, one can contemplate the baroque Sacrarium, with two spacious rooms surrounded by different chapels in which one can see large religious images. The decoration is completed with columns and reredos with gold embellishments.

Continuing our route through Rascafría, we reach to **Las Presillas** where we can enjoy a swim in its natural pools. A little bit forward we find the **Mirador de los Robledos**, from which we can enjoy a good panoramic view of the valley. We turn back in order to take the same road M-604, which will lead us to **Cotos**. This drive is of a wonderful beauty, especially the first days of spring, in which the green colour of the meadows contrasts with the white colour of the snowed mountains.

San Lorenzo de El Escorial

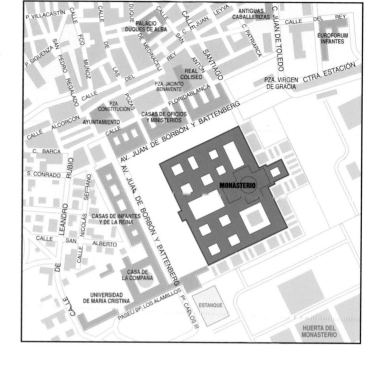

San Lorenzo de El Escorial

We take exit 42 of the N-VI and, after driving for thirteen kilometres, we reach El Escorial. Once inside, we situate ourselves in the old part of the town, where we can see important buildings of historical and artistic interest (16th-18th centuries). But, without doubt, the most important element of this visit is El Escorial Monastery.

Real Monasterio de San Lorenzo de El Escorial

Philip II commissioned this impressive building. The initial construction works were planned by Juan Bautista de Toledo in 1563, and lasted twenty-one years.

Tapestry Museum and Architecture Museum

We start the visit to this great building admiring beautiful tapestries of the series *Los Paños de Oro* (beginning of the 16th century). Before leaving the tapestry halls, we will be able to contemplate the great canvass *El martirio de San Mauricio y la legión Tebana* (16th century) commissioned to El Greco by Philip II.

Architecture Museum

This large hall is divided in two long corridors. To the left, one can see scale models, drawings and plans of El Escorial. In the right corridor, we find the **Sala de Herramientas** (Tool Hall). Here one can see numerous tools such as loading pots, quarry tools, trowels…, etc. At the end of the hall, there are wooden cranes, with

93

Monastery of El Escorial

Monastery of El Escorial

thick ropes and iron pincers, with which the big heavy stones were transported.

Art Gallery
The king Philip II was a great fan of art and painting, which moved him to collect a great number of oils painted by known artists. We will hereby expose the most relevant ele-

ments of this museum. The first things we see are the paintings (oils on panel, 16th century) of Michel Coxcie, one of Philip II favourite painters. Next, we will proceed to another hall where we will be able to see Flemish painting of the 17th century, in particular a great canvass by Paul Van der Meulen representing the passing of the Royal Family through San Sebastián. This hall leads us to another, where we can see Italian paintings of the 16th century, among which we find paintings by Luca Cambiaso, Tiziano or Veronés. Continuing with our visit, we reach a room where the "Master Pieces of Philip II Collection" are exposed. In this room, we see large oil paintings: *The Annunciation* of Paolo Veronés, *La decapitación de Santiago* of Juan Fernández Navarrete, *The Descent from the Cross* of Michel Coxcie. Before leaving this room we can see one of Roger Van Der Weyden's most important paintings, *Calvary* (15th century). In the last section of this useum, we can visit rooms with paintings by: Ribera, Zurbarán, Alonso Cano or Claudio Coello. From this last painter, we would like to highlight his portraits of *Mariana de Austria* and *Mariana de Neoburgo*. We will end our visit with the room dedicated to the Italian painter of the 17th century, Luca Giordano, where one can see works such as *The Doubt of Saint Thomas* or *The Adoration of the Magi,* among others. Crossing a beautiful colonnaded patio and climbing some stairs, we reach the **Sala de Morteros**, which, after traversing some long corridors, leads us to the **Sala de Batallas**. This long gallery is decorated with paintings in fresco (in the walls) representing war motives. A 16th century dome completes the decoration.

Palacio de los Austrias
Going down some stairs we arrive at the

area where the lounges and rooms belonging to the Palace of the Austrian Dynasty are located. In one of the first rooms of this set, a "realejo" organ from the 16th century catches our attention. Passing through a small vestibule, where we can see a sedan chair of Philip II, we enter the **Sala de Audiencias Ordinarias**, also called the **Portrait Hall**. Here we can see paintings of important members of the Spanish House of Austria, signed by painters as well known as Carreño or Claudio Coello. Also in this

Monastery of El Escorial

View of the Monastery Gardens

View of the Monastery of El Escorial from the
Casa de Oficios

room, we can see the folding chairs, made in China, that Philip II used to rest his sick leg, since he had gout. Passing by a gallery, from which we can contemplate the **Gardens of El Escorial**, we reach the **King's Antechamber**, which was formerly used as Philip II dinning-room. Next, we enter another room where we can see a portrait of Philip II as an old man. In front of this pain-

ting is the alcove where Philip II died in the year 1598. This room is decorated with Flemish tapestries of the 16th century and period furniture.

We will leave these royal rooms behind, and stepping down some stairs we will reach one of the most striking areas of El Escorial monastery.

Royal Pantheon

This 17th century pantheon is built in marble. You need to go down some stairs until you reach a circular room where the remains of the kings of Spain, from Charles I to Alphonso XIII, find their rest. The whole room (its three levels) is surrounded by royal sepulchres. Beside the beautiful marble, the room is also decorated with golden bronze pieces. We climb the stairs again to continue through the **Panteón de Infantes** (in total nine rooms filled with sepulchres). Nearly at the end of this route, one finds the **Mausoleo de los Párvulos** placed in the centre, where there are many niches corresponding to infant princes throughout history.

We leave the pantheons climbing some stairs that will take us to the **Salas Capitulares**. And then we will change of atmosphere as we enter the **Sala Vicarial**, where one can see wonderful paintings in fresco (16th century) in the dome of the hall. In this room we can also contemplate oils of religious content by Ribera or El Greco. We continue with the **Sala Prioral** (similar to the former), where paintings by Tiziano and Tintoretto are hung (16th-17th centuries), with the outstanding large canvass of *The Last Supper by Tiziano*.
After traversing some long corridors, where we can see great mural paintings, we leave the building in order to visit the Basilica and the Library.

The Basilica

Placing ourselves in the great **Patio de Reyes**, we enter the temple. The whole church is surrounded with chapels and religious paintings (16th century). In the altar's central area, the great altarpiece stands out.

It was made according to a model by Juan de Herrera (in the middle of the 16th century). The organs, situated to both sides of the premises, complete the decoration of this great building, together with the excellent fresco paintings of the dome made by Luca Giordano.

The Library

This beautiful room is decorated with fresco paintings in the ceiling. The walls are lined with wooden bookcases, which preserve books of great worth such as the illuminated manuscripts, considered true works of art.

View of the Monastery of El Escorial from the Casita del Infante

99

From Chinchón to Aranjuez

12

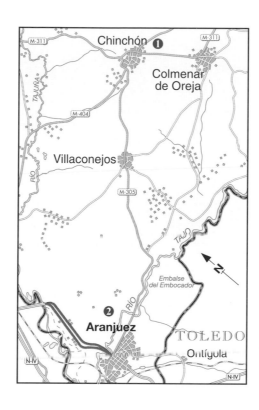

❶ *Chinchón*
❷ *Aranjuez*

Plaza Mayor of Chinchón

We will start this route taking the exit in kilometre twenty-one (N-III) in the direction of Morata de Tajuña-Chinchón and, after four kilometres, we take the road M-311, which will take us (24 km) to Chinchón.

Chinchón

Going down Calle Teniente Ortiz de Zárate, we will see Restaurant posters and advertisements that will guide us towards the Plaza Mayor. Without doubt the greatest attraction of Chinchón is its gastronomic offer and its Plaza Mayor. This important square (15th-17th centuries) is surrounded by numerous wooden balconies from which one can enjoy the traditional Castilian cooking (most part of the balco-

nies are the dining halls of the restaurants that surround the square). Chinchón's Plaza Mayor is one of the most picturesque squares of the Community of Madrid. The Town Hall and the Tourist Office are also located in it. Next to the square, we can see the Church of Our Lady of the Assumption (16th-17th centuries), which has a mixture of several styles with the initial gothic style as prevalent.

We will now take the road M-305 to Aranjuez.

Aranjuez

The **Prince Gardens** are first thing we will see, and they will be accompanying us until we reach the urban centre (3 km).

Plaza Mayor of Chinchón

Placing ourselves inside the town, the Real Sitio y Villa de Aranjuez, we will start our visit by the most important building of the city.

The Royal Palace

It is situated in a peaceful place surrounded by the **Island Gardens** and **The Parterre**

Garden. Philip II commissioned the construction of the palace (16th century) to the architect Juan Bautista de Toledo.

Walk around the Palace

Before starting our visit through the royal lounges, we can see old carriages in one of

Royal Palace of Aranjuez

the corridors that lead inside the elegant building.

The visit will properly start in a hall with a large number of small paintings, most of them made with Indian ink on rice paper. This room leads us to the royal lounges, where one can admire the beautiful **Smoking Room**, the **Arab Room** or the **Chinese Porcelain Room**. After visiting the private lounges, we proceed with our itinerary through rooms of great beauty, similar to those found in the Royal Palace of Madrid: the **State Dining Room** and the **Throne Room**. This last (even though smaller and without golden lions) is nearly a replica of the one in the capital: red velvet decoration, rock crystal lamps..., etc.

After traversing a small room where one

Aranjuez, Casa del Labrador

can see pieces corresponding to the Royal Pharmacy (18th-19th centuries), we move to the **Hall of Children Furniture** where royal cradles, little chairs, and other pieces of children furniture made in wood and decorated with golden motives are exhibited. We continue the visit through the inside of the royal building, and we reach a series of rooms that contain uniforms, complements, and etiquette clothing of the time. The velvet and silk cloaks, such as the *Manto Real de las Reinas de España* (19th century), deserve special attention.

In the last section of this visit, we can see royal portraits and period furniture, with an outstanding armchair that belonged to Ferdinand VII. The last rooms lead us to the **Game Room**, where we can see an interesting portable gym set made in wood and lined with red velvet, and some wood bicycles.

Island Gardens and The Parterre Garden

Having finished the visit around the Royal Palace, there is nothing better than continuing our itinerary throughout these beautiful gardens. This large landscaped space is situated next to the Royal Palace, and throughout our walk we will be able to see numerous statues and fountains that, together with the green areas and the river, contribute to make of this place one of Aranjuez's most outstanding landscaped zones.

Royal Palace of Aranjuez

Royal Casa del Labrador

Island Gardens and The Parterre Gardens

After visiting the palace and the gardens, we recommend continuing the visit in the "microtrain" ("Chiquitrén") of Aranjuez. The tourist ride around Aranjuez departs from the Royal Palace, traversing Aranjuez and the inside of the Prince Gardens. Throughout the ride we will find numerous places of interest, among which are:

– The Garden of Isabel II (19th century)
– The House of the Infantas (18th century)
– The Royal Church of Saint Anthony (18th century)
– The Church of Alpajés (17th-18th centuries)

– The Prince Garden, and the smaller palace Real Casa del Labrador (18th-19th centuries)
– The Museum-Bullfighting Ring (18th-19th centuries)

After the "Chiquitrén" trip, one can stop for thirty minutes in the Prince Gardens.

We also recommend the visit on board Aranjuez' tourist boat, which will navigate the waters of the Tajo River, allowing you to enjoy the natural setting of the Prince Gardens.

Alcalá de Henares

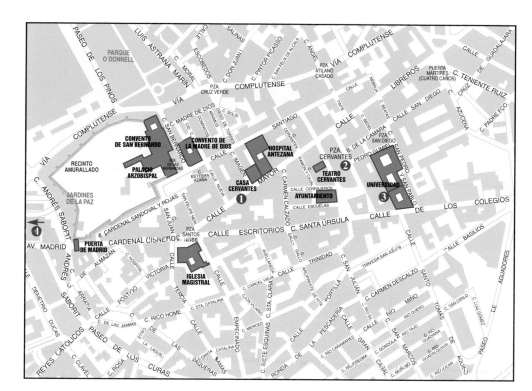

13

- ❶ *Calle Mayor*
- ❷ *Plaza de Cervantes*
- ❸ *Universidad*
- ❹ *Ciudad Romana*

Calle Mayor

After passing Torrejón de Ardoz, and very close to Madrid, we will encounter Alcalá de Henares, a university town declared World Heritage since 1998.

Calle Mayor

Placing ourselves in the old part of the town, we will begin our visit taking Calle Mayor, one of the longest colonnaded streets in Spain. The walk along this picturesque street is pleasant and, soon after we start, we find buildings of historical interest such as the **Hospital of Our Lady of Mercy or of Antezana** (15th century), which has a beautiful Castilian patio, or the **Museo Casa Natal de Miguel de Cervantes** (16th century). The author of *Don Quixote* was born in this house, where we can see an extraordinary collection of period furniture and other editions of *Don Quixote* in different languages. At the end of Calle Mayor, we find the Plaza de los Santos Niños where we will see the impressive building of the **Iglesia Catedral Magistral de los Santos**

109

Archbishop's Palace in Alcalá de Henares

Plaza de Cervantes

Plaza de las Bernardas

Justo y Pastor. Going down Calle Cardenal Cisneros, we will arrive at **Puerta de Madrid** and the walled enclosure of the city. Going up Calle del Cardenal Sandoval y Rojas we will see the **Archbishop's Palace** (14th-18th centuries), the **Monastery of Saint Bernard** (17th century) and the **Regional Archaeology Museum** (old Convent of the Mother of God).

Plaza de Cervantes

We will go up Calle Mayor to contemplate again the long street with arcades that will take us to **Plaza Mayor de Alcalá de Henares** (Cervantes' Plaza). In this *plaza*, it is located the **Corral de Comedias** (or open air theatre) and the **Town Hall**, the old Convent of Saint Charles, 17th century,

Previous page:
University of Alcalá de Henares

inside which one can see exhibitions of period objects and magnificent lounges such as the **Salón de Plenos** (or Plenary Session Hall) (19th century).

Universidad de Alcalá de Henares

Adjoining Plaza de Cervantes, one finds the city's most emblematic building: The University of Alcalá. It was founded by Cardinal Cisneros in the year 1499, and it is one of the best university ensembles of European Renaissance. After visiting some of the building's patios, we go into the chapel, constructed in different styles, especially Mudejar. Inside we find the marble sepulchre of Cardinal Cisneros. Another important room inside the university is the **Auditorium** (or **Paraninfo**), where every year Their Majesties the kings of Spain grant the Cervantes Prize for Literature.

Roman Town

We can also visit the **Roman City of Complutum** and the **House of Hippolytus**.

Guided tours depart from the Plaza Mayor of Alcalá by bus, which will allow you to visit other places of interest in Alcalá de Henares.

Instituto Cervantes (Church of Santa María)

From Navacerrada to Manzanares El Real

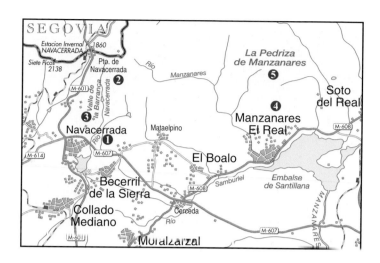

- ❶ Navacerrada
- ❷ Puerto de Navacerrada
- ❸ Valle de la Barranca
- ❹ Manzanares El Real
- ❺ La Pedriza

Navacerrada

As we arrive to Collado Villalba, we take the exit in the N-VI in the direction of Puerto de Navacerrada (N-601). Once in the A-road and after driving for nine kilometres, we will see the reservoir and soon after (2 km) we will reach this well-known town of the Sierra of Madrid. Without more ado, we will go up the **Puerto de Navacerrada** (1800 m), from where we will enjoy wonderful views of the sierra, especially during the snowy season.
The Navacerrada Pass also provides skiing slopes and ski lifts, skiing school, hotels and restaurants.

Valle de la Barranca

In the town's outskirts (3 km), we will find the exit that will lead us to this great natural space where the hotel of La Barranca is located. In front of the hotel starts a guided hike to practice trekking. During this route we will be accompanied by the Navacerrada River and the beautiful pinewoods that surround the valley. In the hotel's surroundings there are meadows with picnic tables from where you can also enjoy nice views of the reservoir and the town of Navacerrada.

Manzanares El Real

In order to arrive to Manzanares we will need to take the road M-607 in the direction of Cerceda and, once there, we will head to Soto del Real (M-608), and after driving for six kilometres we will arrive to Manzanares El Real.
The Castle (14th-15th centuries) is surrounded by green areas. We will first go up a lit-

Castle of Manzanares El Real

▲

Sculpture in Puerto de Navacerrada

▶

Church of Nuestra Señora de las Nieves, Manzanares El Real

tle slope that will lead us to the building; once inside, the atmosphere transports us to a different epoch as we admire the furniture, tapestries and suits of armour that decorate the vestibule.

Climbing some stairs we start visiting the castle's different rooms, among which the **Congress Hall** and the **Library**, accessed by a staircase situated in a cylindrical tower, deserve special attention. Moreover, the visitor will enjoy the wonderful views that this important building offers, especially from the gallery and the battlements. From

them one can see the **Reservoir of Santillana**, the **Iglesia de Nuestra Señora de las Nieves** (15th century) and **La Pedriza**, the last stop of this itinerary.

La Pedriza

Near the town of Manzanares El Real, we find the spectacular rock formations of La Pedriza. The visit is really worthwhile, but those who wish to enjoy such beautiful setting would need to do it by foot.

Toledo

Toledo 15

1 Puerta de la Bisagra
2 Puerta de Alfonso VI
3 Puente de Alcántara
4 Puente de San Martín
5 Alcázar
6 Hospital de Santa Cruz
7 Hospital de Tavera o Afuera
8 Catedral
9 Casa Museo de El Greco
10 Sinagoga del Tránsito. Museo Sefardí
11 Sinagoga de Santa María la Blanca
12 Monasterio de San Juan de los Reyes
13 El Embarcadero

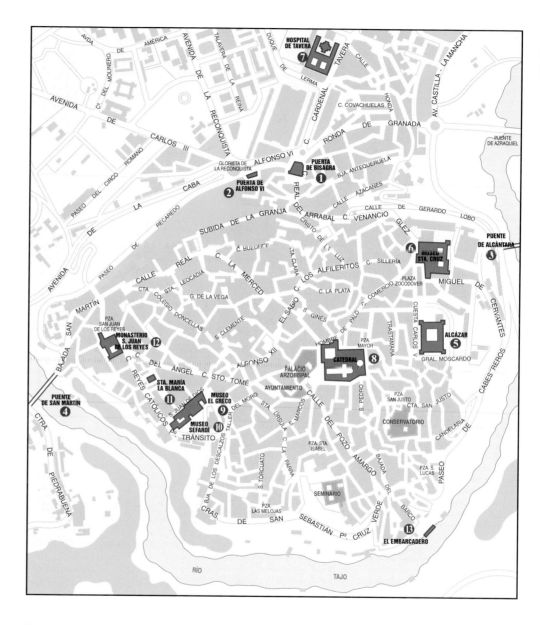

Without doubt the city of Toledo is the most visited of the whole Autonomous Community of Castilla-La Mancha. The old part of the town (of great historical and artistic interest) is a walled enclosure, which has been declared World Heritage.

Entering the city

The road N-401 leads us directly to the doors of the historical centre of Toledo, and from there we can see the walls of this important city. The walls, which already exis-

*Detail of the Monastery of
San Juan de los Reyes*

ted in the Roman period, were reconstructed by the Arabs, and today still have numerous well-preserved towers and doors, like the **Puerta de la Bisagra** (with a great court of arms) and the **Puerta de Alfonso VI** (with landscaped areas).

The Bridges and Tajo River

Making a detour around the outside of the walled city, we meet the **Alcántara Bridge** and, lying at its base, the Tajo riverbed, which also surrounds the city. This great bridge (of

Roman origin) provided access to the town and had a court of arms with three doors (of which only one remains). To one side of the bridge and at the top of a hill, it is situated the **Castle of San Servando**, from where one can enjoy a beautiful view of Toledo. Another bridge that deserves to be mentioned is the **Bridge of San Martín**, which is located on the other side of the city and which is also part of the walled enclosure.

Bridge of San Martín

Walls of Toledo and Bridge of Alcántara

Plaza de San Juan de los Reyes

Heading toward El Greco Museum

Street of the old part of the city, with the cathedral in the background

El Alcázar

Together with the Cathedral, this is the highest building of the old part of the town and it offers one of the most typical pictures of Toledo. The building served as praetorian palace (3rd century) during Roman times and as fortress-palace for the Arabs. Inside the Alcázar we find today the **Army Museum**.

▲

Detail from one of the buildings of Toledo's historical part of the city

The Hospitals:

— **Hospital de Santa Cruz**. Ancient hospital (plateresque style, 16th century) turned into a museum, which exhibits El Greco paintings.

— **Hospital de Tavera o Afuera**. Ancient hospital (renaissance style, 16th century) which now shelters the **Museo de Tavera**, which contains important paintings by El Greco, Carreño, Ribera and Tintoretto.

The Cathedral

Located in the centre of the old part of the town, this cathedral is one of the biggest in Spain. This great building of gothic style began to be built in the year 1226 and it was not finished until the end of the 15th century. The inside of the cathedral is of great beauty, with numerous chapels that deserve to be visited, together with the **Museo de Arte Religioso**.

Walk around its streets

There are so many monuments, buildings, and streets of historical and artistic interest, that one can consider the whole of Toledo a big museum. From the whole city we would like to highlight the **Jewish Quarter** (or **Judería**) composed by the streets: Calle de los Reyes Católicos, Calle de San Juan de Dios and Paseo del Tránsito.

Calle de San Juan de Dios
The first thing we encounter in this street (as we go down to Calle de los Reyes Católicos) is the **Casa Museo de El Greco**, where we will be able to see period furniture and paintings by El Greco.
One step away, we find the lovely **Sinagoga del Tránsito** (14th century), inside which we can visit the **Museo Sefardí de Toledo**.

Paseo del Tránsito
Leaving the Sinagogue, a peaceful park awaits us, el Paseo del Tránsito, offering us wonderful views over the Tajo River.

Calle de Reyes Católicos
Continuing our walk along Calle de los Reyes Católicos, we find the **Sinagoga de Santa María la Blanca** (smaller than the Sinagoga del Tránsito, 13th century) and, at the end of the street, we encounter the **Monasterio de San Juan de los Reyes** (gothic-mudejar style, 15th century), whose construction was commissioned by the Catholic Kings.

The Pier
With this picturesque setting we arrive to the full stop of this beautiful excursion through Toledo. This place is inhabited by a large number of ducks, which swim next to the Tajo River banks. The Pier has a square boat, which will take us slowly to the other riverbank. This boat is not run by an engine, and neither does it make use of oars, it is, however, moved by an operative that turns a crank around so that the boat can slowly glide over a rail, and so one can deliberately contemplate the beautiful scenery that surrounds the Tajo River.

"The Pier" next Tajo River

Practical Data

TELEPHONES OF INTEREST

Information about Madrid: ☎ 010

Tourist Office of the Town Hall of Madrid: Plaza Mayor, ☎ 91 588 16 36

Community of Madrid: ☎ 012

Tourist Office of the Community of Madrid: Puerta de Toledo, ☎ 91 364 18 76. Duque de Medinaceli, 2, ☎ 91 429 49 51

Telephone Information: ☎ 11818

EMERGENCIES

Emergencies in general: ☎ 112

Police: ☎ 091 y 092

Fire Brigade: ☎ 080

Samur (Medical Emergencies): ☎ 092

HOW TO MOVE

BY PLANE

Barajas Airport: 12 km. from Madrid with bus service and subway to the centre of the city (information ☎ 902 400 500).

From the underground station of Nuevos Ministerios there is a direct line connecting with the airport, with luggage check-in.

From the bus terminal of the Plaza del Descubrimiento leaves a bus that takes between 30 to 60 minutes –depending on the traffic– in reaching the airport.

BY TRAIN

Chamartin station: ☎ 91 315 99 76. Trains to Europe, suburban and regional trains to the north of Spain.

Atocha station: ☎ 91 506 68 46. Trains to Portugal, south of Spain, AVE (high-speed train) and suburban trains.

Príncipe Pío station: ☎ 91 468 42 00. Suburban trains.

BY BUS

Sur station: ☎ 91 468 42 00. The majority of bus companies are located in this station.

Auto-Res: ☎ 91 551 72 00. Buses with destination: Extremadura, Castellón, Cuenca, Salamanca, Valencia, Vigo and Zamora.

Continental: ☎ 91 745 63 00. Buses with destination: Álava, Almería, Burgos, Cantabria, Granada, Guadalajara, Guipúzcoa, La Rioja, Málaga, Navarra, Soria, Toledo and Vizcaya.

La Sepulvedana: ☎ 91 530 48 00. Buses to Segovia.

BY TUBE AND BUS INSIDE THE CITY

Madrid's bus network (EMT ☎ 91 406 88 10), has 179 lines functioning from 6 h to 24 h with an interval of 3 to 15 minutes (depending on the schedule). There are also nightlines, known as "búhos" (owls), which function from 0 h to 5 h every 30 minutes, and from 3 h every hour, and which leave from Plaza de Cibeles in various directions.

The underground system (☎ 902 444 403),

has 11 lines which function from 6 h to 1,30 h, every 3-5 minutes till 23 h and from then onwards every 10 minutes.

The ticket used for the underground and the bus is the same and has no distance limit, it can be bought single or with 10 rides for an economical price in underground stations or EMT offices.

TAXIS

Tele-Taxi: ☎ 91 445 90 08

Radio-Taxi: ☎ 91 447 51 80

Radio-Taxi Independiente: ☎ 91 405 12 13

Radio-Teléfono taxi: ☎ 91 547 82 00

WHERE TO SLEEP

FIVE-STAR HOTELS

AC Palacio de Santo Mauro: Zurbano, 36. ☎ 91 319 69 00

A Park Hyatt, Villa Magna: Paseo de la Castellana, 22. ☎ 91 587 12 34.

Husa Princesa: Pricesa, 40. ☎ 91 542 21 00

Miguel Ángel Occidental: Miguel Ángel, 31. ☎ 91 442 00 22

Palace: Pza. de las Cortes, 7; ☎ 91 360 80 00

Ritz: Pza. de la Lealtad, 5; ☎ 91 521 28 57

Tryp Monte Real: Arroyofresno, 17 (Pta. de Hierro). ☎ 91 316 21 40.

Wellington: Velázquez, 8. ☎ 91 575 44 00

FOUR-STAR HOTELS:

NH Alcalá: Alcalá, 66. ☎ 91 435 10 60

Arosa: Salud, 21. ☎ 91 532 16 00

Barajas: Avda. de Logroño, 305. ☎ 91 747 77 00

Eurobuilding: Padre Damián, 23. ☎ 91 345 45 00

Carlton: Paseo de las Delicias, 26. ☎ 91 539 71 00

Castellana Inter-Continental. Paseo de la Castellana, 49. ☎ 91 310 02 00

Chamartín: Agustín de Foxá. ☎ 91 334 49 00

Colón: Pez Volador, 9-11. ☎ 91 573 59 00

Convención: O'Donnell, 53. ☎ 91 574 68 00

Cuzco: Paseo de la Castellana, 133. ☎ 91 556 06 00

Emperador: Gran Vía, 53. ☎ 91 547 28 00

Emperatriz: López de Hoyos, 4. ☎ 91 563 80 88

Gaudí: Gran Vía, 9; ☎ 91 531 22 22

Gran Atlanta: Comandante Zorita, 34. ☎ 91 553 59 00

Gran Hotel Conde Duque: Pza. del Conde Valle de Suchil, 5. ☎ 91 447 70 00

Meliá Castilla: Capitán Haya, 43. ☎ 91 567 50 00

Novotel Madrid Campo de las Naciones: Avda. Recinto Ferial Juan Carlos I. ☎ 91 721 18 18

Suecia: Marqués de Casa Riera, 4. ☎ 91 531 69 00

Villa Real: Pza. de las Cortes, 10. ☎ 91 420 37 67

COMMUNITY OF MADRID

Alcalá de Henares: Green Cisneros (***), Paseo de Pastrana, 32; ☎ 91 883 19 95

Buitrago del Lozoya: Posada de los Vientos, Encerradero, 2; ☎ 91 869 91 95 (in La Acebeda, 4 km. from Buitrago)

Chinchón: Parador Nacional de Turismo de Chinchón (****): Generalísimo, 1;
☎ 91 894 0836

Navacerrada: Hotel Arcipreste de Hita (****), A-road N-601, km 12;
☎ 91 856 01 25

Hotel La Barranca (***), Valle de la Barranca, s/n; ☎ 91 856 00 00

Navalcarnero: Hotel Real Villa de Navalcarnero (***). Paseo de San Cosme, s/n; ☎ 91 811 24 93

Rascafría: Hotel Santa María del Paular (****), B-road M-604, km 26,5;
☎ 91 869 01 11

San Lorenzo de El Escorial: Hotel Victoria Palace (****), Juan de Toledo, 4;
☎ 91 890 15 11

WHERE TO EAT

TRADITIONAL COOKING

Botín: Cuchilleros, 7; ☎ 91 366 42 17

Café de Oriente: Pza. de Oriente, 2;
☎ 91 541 39 74

Carmencita: Libertad, 16; ☎ 91 531 66 12

Casa Ciriaco: Mayor, 84; ☎ 91 548 06 20

Casa Lucio: Cava Baja, 35; ☎ 91 365 32 52

Casa Paco: Puerta Cerrada, 11;
☎ 91 366 31 66

Casa Patas: Cañizares, 10; ☎ 91 369 04 96

La Bola: Bola, 5; ☎ 91 547 69 30

La Tahona: Capitán Haya, 21;
☎ 91 555 04 41

Lhardy: Carrera de San Jerónimo, 8;
☎ 91 521 33 85

Julián de Tolosa: Cava Baja, 18;
☎ 91 365 82 10

Taberna del Alabardero: Felipe V, 6;
☎ 91 547 25 77

"AUTEUR" COOKING

El Amparo: Puigcerdá, 8; ☎ 91 431 64 56

Balzac: Moreto, 7; ☎ 91 420 01 77

Combarro: José Ortega y Gasset, 40;
☎ 91 577 82 72

Club 31: Alcalá, 58; ☎ 91 531 00 92

Cabo Mayor: Juan Ramón Jiménez, 37;
☎ 91 350 87 76

Currito: Casa de Campo. Pabellón de Vizcaya; ☎ 91 464 57 04

El Cenador del Prado: Prado, 4;
☎ 91 429 15 61

El fogón de Zein. Cardenal Cisneros, 49;
☎ 91 593 33 20

El Mentidero de la Villa: Santo Tomé, 6;
☎ 91 308 12 85

Horcher: Alfonso XII, 6;
☎ 91 522 07 31

Jockey: Amador de los Ríos, 6
☎ 91 319 24 35

La Ancha: Príncipe de Vergara, 204;
☎ 91 563 89 77

O'Pazo: Reina Mercedes, 20;
☎ 91 534 37 48

Pedro Larumbe: Serrano, 61;
☎ 91 575 11 12

Príncipe de Viana: Manuel de Falla, 5;
☎ 91 457 15 49

Viridiana: Juan de Mena, 14;
☎ 91 531 52 22

Zalacaín: Álvarez de Baena, 4;
☎ 91 561 48 40

PUBS

Almendro, 13: Almendro, 13;
☎ 91 365 42 52

Don Pedro: Don Pedro, 20;
☎ 91 366 21 74

El Anciano: Bailén, 19. ☎ 91 559 53 32

España Cañí: Pza. del Ángel, 4

La Bardemcilla: Cristo, 2; ☎ 91 541 41 12

La Dolores: Pza. de Jesús, 4;
☎ 91 429 22 43

La Venencia: Echegaray, 7; ☎ 91 429 73 13

Taberna de Antonio Sánchez: Mesón de
Paredes, 13; ☎ 91 539 78 26

Taberna de Don Alonso: Alonso Cano, 64;
☎ 91 533 52 49

Taberna del Avapiés: Lavapiés, 5;
☎ 91 539 26 50

Taberna del Pirata: Quintana, 10;
☎ 91 542 99 51

CAFÉS

Barbieri: Ave María, 45. Open everyday
from 15 h to 2 h. Fridays and Saturdays till
3 h.

Comercial: Glorieta de Bilbao, 7. Open
everyday from 8 h to1 h. Fridays and
Saturdays till 2,30 h.

De los Austrias: Pza. de Ramales, 1. Open
everyday from 17 h to 1,30 h. Fridays and
Saturdays till 3 h.

Del Foro: San Andrés, 38. Open everyday
from19 h to 3 h. Fridays and Saturdays till
4 h.

Gijón: Paseo de Recoletos, 21. Open
everyday from 8 h to 1,30 h. Saturdays till
2 h.

Madrid: Mesón de Paños, 6. Everyday from
15,30 h to 2,30 h.

Moderno: Pza. de las Comendadoras, 1.
Open everyday from 15 h to 2 h. Fridays
and Saturdays till 3 h.

Del Nuncio: Nuncio, 12. Everyday from
12,30 h a 2,30 h. Fridays and Saturdays till
3,30 h.

Oriental: San Bernardino, 1. Open everyday
from 19 h to 3 h.

Salón del Prado: Prado, 4. Everyday from
14 h to 2 h.

BARS

Alemana: Pza. de Santa Ana, 6. Open from
10,30 h to 24,30 h. Fridays and Saturdays
till 2 h. Tuesdays closed.

Bulevar: Santa Teresa, 2. Open everyday
from 12,30 h to 2 h. Fridays and Saturdays
till 4 h.

De la Villa: San Mateo, 28. Open everyday
from 18 h to 24,30 h.

Santa Ana: Pza. de Santa Ana, 6. Open
everyday from 10 h a 1,30 h. Fridays and
Saturdays till 2,30 h.

Santa Bárbara: Pza. de Santa Bárbara, 8.
Open everyday from 11,30 h to
23,30 h.

COMMUNITY OF MADRID

Alcalá de Henares: Hostería del Estudiante,
Colegios, 3; ☎ 91 888 03 30

Aranjuez: Casa José, Abastos, 32;
☎ 91 892 02 04

Buitrago del Lozoya: El Arco, Arco, 6;
☎ 91 868 09 11 (in Villavieja del Lozoya,
6 km. from Buitrago)

Chinchón: Mesón de la Virreina, Pza. Mayor,
28; ☎ 91 894 00 15

Manzanares El Real: Azaya, Muñoz Grandes, 7; ☎ 91 857 33 95 (in Mataelpino 7 km. from Manzanares).

Navacerrada: Asador Felipe, Calle del Mayo, 3; ☎ 91 853 10 41

Navalcarnero: Hostería de las Monjas, Glorieta de la Iglesia, 1; ☎ 91 811 18 19

Pinilla del Valle: El Corralón del Embalse, Presa, 26; ☎ 91 869 34 38

Rascafría: Santa María del Paular y Don Lope, B-road M-604, km. 26,5; ☎ 91 869 10 11

San Lorenzo de El Escorial: Charolés, Floridablanca, 24; ☎ 91 890 59 75

La Buganvilla, Timoteo Padrós, 16 (Hotel Botánico); ☎ 91 890 78 79

HOLIDAYS

MADRID

Cabalgata de Reyes: January 5. Spectacular parade dedicated to children on the eve of Three Kings' Day.

San Antón: January 17. Blessing of domestic animals in the church of St. Antón in Calle Hortaleza. After the blessing, it is customary to eat the typical "panecillos del Santo".

Carnaval: In February. Carnaval kicks off with a parade of floats along Paseo de la Castellana and the festivities end with the famous "Burial of the Sardine".

Feria de Abril: In April. A replica of the Seville Fair. It takes place in Las Ventas.

Fiestas de la Comunidad: May 2. Mass in the morning in the Florida cemetery in memory of the May 2, 1808 victims of the War of Independence. There are dances, concerts, and performances.

San Isidro: May 8-15. Patron Saint of Madrid. There are concerts, fairs where people dance the traditional "chotis" (typical dance from Madrid), bullfights, and popular fiestas at the Hermitage of San Isidro, where it is customary to drink water from the fountain of this saint. During this time, the Antique Book Fair is also celebrated.

San Antonio de la Florida: June 9-13. Originally this was a celebration in which dressmakers would go to the Hermitage of San Antonio and would pray to the Saint to find them a boyfriend. There is music, dance and concerts.

Virgen del Carmen: July 1-15. Very popular fiestas in honour of the Patron Saint of Chamberí.

San Lorenzo, San Cayetano and La Paloma: August 6-15. The popular quarter of Lavapiés celebrates fiestas in honour of San Lorenzo and San Cayetano, which are preceded by the fiestas of La Paloma, the unofficial Patron Saint of Madrid. Contests, music, dances, concerts...

La Melonera: September 8. It takes place in the Hermitage of Virgen del Puerto.

La Almudena: November 9. The Virgin of La Almudena is the Patron Saint of Madrid. Mass is celebrated in the Cathedral of La Almudena.

Nochevieja: (New Years' Eve). There is a mass concentration of people in Puerta del Sol, to ring in the New Year with the traditional "12 grapes". It is customary to eat one grape at each chime of the most famous clock in Spain.

COMMUNITY OF MADRID

Alcalá de Henares: San Bartolomé. August 24. Infant Saints Justo and Pastor; August 6. Virgen del Val, September's third Sunday.

Aranjuez: San Fernando, May 30.

Buitrago del Lozoya: Ntra. Señora de la Asunción, August 14 16. Cristo de los Esclavos, September 15.

Chinchón: Virgen de Gracia and San Roque. August 15-21. Santiago, July 25. Virgen del Rosario, September's third Sunday.

Manzanares El Real: Ntra. Señora de la Peña Sacra. Pentecost's first Monday. Santísimo Cristo de la Nava, September 14. Ntra. Señora de las Nieves. August 5.

Navacerrada: Nativity of Our Lady. September 8. San Antonio de Padua, July 13.

Navalcarnero: Our Lady of Conception, September 7. San Isidro Labrador. May 15.

Rascafría: Virgin of the Assumption. August 15. San Andrés. November 30.

San Lorenzo de El Escorial: San Lorenzo, August 10.

MUSEUMS AND MONUMENTS

General Information about Museums: ☎ 098

Aeronáutica y Astronáutica: Ctra. de Extremadura km. 10,5. ☎ 91 509 16 90. Open from 10 h to 14 h. Mondays closed.

Africano: Arturo Soria, 101. ☎ 91 415 80 00.

América: Avda. de los Reyes Católicos, 6. ☎ 91 543 94 37. Open from Tuesday to Saturday, from 10 h to 15 h. Sundays and holidays from 10 h to 14,30 h. Mondays closed.

Ángel Nieto: Pedro del Bosch, s/n. ☎ 91 468 02 24

Antropológico: Juan de Herrera, 2. ☎ 91 549 71 50.

Arqueológico Nacional: Serrano, 13. ☎ 91 577 79 12. Open from Tuesday to Saturday, from 9,30 h to 20,30 h. Sundays, from 9,30 h to 14,30 h.

Arte Moderno (Casón del Buen Retiro): Felipe IV, 28. ☎ 91 420 24 15. Open from 9 h to 19 h. Sundays and holidays from 9 h to 14 h.

Arte del Siglo XIX: Felipe IV, 28. ☎ 91 330 28 00. Open from 9 h to 19 h. Sundays and holidays from 9 h to 14 h.

Artes Decorativas: Montalbán, 12. ☎ 91 532 68 45. Open from 9,30 h to 15 h. Saturdays, Sundays and holidays from 10 h to 14 h. Mondays closed.

Artes y Tradiciones Populares: Ctra. de Colmenar Viejo, km 15. Universidad Autónoma de Madrid. ☎ 91 397 50 00. Open from Monday to Friday, from 11 h to 14 h. Tuesdays and Thursdays from 17 h to 20 h.

Ateneo Científico y Literario: Prado, 21. ☎ 91 429 17 50.

Basílica de San Miguel: San Justo, 4. ☎ 91 548 40 11.

Biblioteca Nacional: Paseo de Recoletos, 20. ☎ 91 580 78 00.

Biblioteca de la Sociedad General de Autores: Fernando VI, 4. ☎ 91 349 95 50.

Bomberos (Fire Brigade): Avda. Pío Felipe, s/n. ☎ 91 478 65 72. Open from 10 h to 13,30 h. Holidays closed.

Calcografía: Alcalá, 13.
☎ 91 532 15 43

Capilla y Pozo de San Isidro: Pza. de San Andrés, 1. ☎ 91 366 74 15.

Carrozas y Carruajes: Paseo de la Virgen del Puerto, s/n. ☎ 91 548 74 15.

Casa de América (Palacio de Linares): Paseo de Recoletos, 2.
☎ 91 549 26 41.

Casa de la Moneda y Timbre: Doctor Esquerdo, 36. ☎ 91 566 65 44. Open from 10 h to 14,30 h, and from 17 h to 19,30 h. Saturdays, Sundays, and holidays from 10 h to14 h. Mondays closed.

Casa de Lope de Vega: Cervantes, 11.
☎ 91 429 92 16.

Centro de Arte Reina Sofía: Santa Isabel, 52. ☎ 91 467 50 62. Open everyday from 10 h to 21 h. Sundays from 10 h to 14,30 h. Tuesdays closed.

Cera (Wax Museum): Paseo de Recoletos, 41. ☎ 91 308 08 25. Open from 10 h to 14,30 h, and from 16,30 h to 20,30 h. Saturdays, Sundays and holidays does not close at midday.

Cerralbo: Ventura Rodríguez, 17.
☎ 91 547 36 46. Open from Tuesday to Saturday, from 9,30 h to 14, 30 h. Sundays from 10 h to 14 h. Mondays closed.

Ciencia y Tecnología: Paseo de las Delicias, 61. ☎ 91 530 31 21.

Ciencias Naturales: José Gutierrez Abascal, 2. ☎ 91 411 13 28. Open from Tuesday to Friday, from 10 h to 18 h. Saturdays from 10 h to 20 h. Mondays, Sundays, and holidays from 10 h to 14,30 h.

Ciudad de Madrid: Príncipe de Vergara, 140. ☎ 91 588 65 99. Open from Tuesday to Friday from 10 h to 14 h and from 16 h to 18 h. Saturdays and Sundays from 10 h to 14 h. Mondays and holidays closed.

Colección de Anatomía: Facultad de Ciencias. ☎ 91 397 48 00.

Colección de la Biblioteca Musical: Conde Duque, 9. ☎ 91 588 57 51.

Colección de Mineralogía (Universidad de Cantoblanco): Facultad de Ciencias, ☎ 91 397 48 00.

Colección Municipal: Pza. de la Villa, 4 y 5. ☎ 91 542 55 12.

Colección Thyssen-Bornemisza: Paseo del Prado, 8. ☎ 91 369 01 51. Open from Tuesday to Sunday from 10 h to 19 h. Mondays closed.

Convento de San Plácido: San Roque, 9.
☎ 91 531 79 99.

Cosmo Caixa: Pintor Murillo, 5. Parque de Andalucía, Alcobendas. ☎ 91 484 52 00. Horario de 10 h a 18 h.

Ejército (Army Museum): Méndez Núñez, 1. ☎ 91 522 06 28. Open from 10 h to 14 h. Mondays closed.

Ermita de San Antonio de la Florida: Glorieta de San Antonio de la Florida, 5.
☎ 91 542 07 22.

Erótico: Doctor Cortezo, 2.
☎ 91 369 39 71.

Escultura al Aire Libre (Open Air Sculpture): underneath the bridge that crosses Paseo de la Castellana, connecting the streets Juan Bravo and Eduardo Dato.

Etnológico y Antropológico: Alfonso XII, 68. ☎ 91 530 64 18. Open from Tuesday to Saturday from 10 h to 19,30 h. Sundays and holidays from 10 h to 14 h. Mondays closed.

Farmacia Hispana: Facultad de Farmacia.
☎ 91 394 17 97.

Farmacia Militar: Embajadores, 75.
☎ 91 539 10 07

Ferrocarril: Paseo de las Delicias, 61.
☎ 902 22 88 22. Open Tuesdays to Sundays from 10 h to 15 h. Mondays closed.

Fundación Casa de Alba (Palacio de Liria): Princesa, 20-22. ☎ 91 547 53 02. Open on Friday morning with appointment.

Geominiero: Ríos Rosas, 23.
☎ 91 349 57 00. Open from Monday to Saturday from 9 h to 14 h. Sundays and holidays closed.

Guardia Civil: Guzmán El Bueno, 110.
☎ 91 534 02 00.

Histórico Minero D. Felipe de Borbón y Grecia: Ríos Rosas, 21.
☎ 91 336 70 17.

Insituto Valencia de Don Juan: Fortuny, 43. ☎ 91 308 18 48.

Interactivo del Libro: Paseo de Recoletos, 20. ☎ 91 580 77 59. Open from 10 h to 21 h. Sundays and holidays from 10 h to 14 h. Mondays closed.

Lázaro Galdiano: Serrano, 122.
☎ 91 561 60 84. Open from 10 h to 14 h. Mondays closed.

Mesonero Romanos: Pza. Mayor, 27.
☎ 91 588 23 87.

Monasterio de la Encarnación: Pza. de la Encarnación, 1. ☎ 91 547 05 10. Open from Tuesday to Saturday from 10,30 h to 12,45 h. Holidays from 11 h to 13,45 h. Monday and Friday afternoons closed.

Monasterio de las Descalzas Reales: Pza. de las Descalzas Reales, 3. ☎ 91 521 14 91. Open from Tuesday to Saturday, from 10,30 h to 12,45 h, and from 16 h to 17,45 h. Holidays from 11 h to 13,45 h. Monday and Friday afternoons closed.

Municipal: Fuencarral, 78. ☎ 91 588 86 72. Open from Tuesday to Friday, from 9 h to 20 h. Saturdays and Sundays from 10 h to 14 h. Mondays and holidays closed.

Museo Naval: Paseo del Prado, 5.
☎ 91 379 52 99. Open from 10,30 h to 13,30 h. Mondays closed.

Observatorio Astronómico (Colección): Alfonso XII, 3. ☎ 91 527 01 07.

Palacio de Cristal: Parque del Retiro.
☎ 91 574 66 14.

Palacio de Velázquez: Parque del Retiro.
☎ 91 573 62 45.

Palacio Real: Bailén, s/n. ☎ 91 559 74 04. Summer schedule (from April to September): from Monday to Saturday, from 9 h to 18 h. Sundays and holidays from 9 h to 15 h. Winter schedule (from October to March): from Monday to Saturday, from 9,30 h to 17 h. Sundays and holidays from 9 h to 14 h.

Panteón de Goya: Gta. de San Antonio de la Florida. ☎ 91 542 07 22.

Panteón de Hombres Ilustres: Julián Gayarre, 3. ☎ 91 542 00 59.

Planetario y Cine IMAX: Parque Tierno Galván. ☎ 91 467 38 98.

Postal y Telecomunicaciones: Montalbán, s/n. ☎ 91 521 65 00.

Prado: Paseo del Prado, s/n. ☎ 91 330 28 00. Open from Tuesday to Saturday, from 9 h to 19 h. Sundays and holidays from 9 h to 14 h. Mondays closed.

Real Academia de Bellas Artes de San Fernando: Alcalá, 13. ☎ 91 522 14 91. Open from Tuesday to Friday, from 9 h to 19 h. Saturdays, Sundays, and Mondays from 9 h to 14 h.

Real Academia de la Historia: León, 21. ☎ 91 429 06 11.

Real Armería (Palacio Real): Bailén, s/n. ☎ 91 542 00 59.

Real Basílica de San Francisco El Grande: San Buenaventura, 1. ☎ 91 365 38 00.

Real Fábrica de Tapices: Fuenterrabía, 2. ☎ 91 434 05 51. Open from 9,30 h to 12,30 h. Saturdays, Sundays and August closed.

Real Jardín Botánico: Pza. de Murillo, 2. ☎ 91 420 30 17. Open from 10 h till sunset.

Real Oficina de Farmacia (Palacio Real): Bailén, s/n. ☎ 91 542 00 59.

Reproducciones Artísticas: Avda. de Juan de Herrera, 2. ☎ 91 549 71 50.

Romántico: San Mateo, 13 ☎ 91 448 10 45. Open from Tuesday to Saturday, from 9 h to 15 h. Sundays and holidays from 10 h to 14 h.

San Antonio Abad: Hortaleza, 63. ☎ 91 521 74 73.

Sorolla: Paseo del General Martínez Campos, 37. ☎ 91 310 15 84. Open everyday from 10 h to 15 h. Sundays from 10 h to 14 h. Mondays closed.

Taurino (Plaza de Toros de Las Ventas): Alcalá, 237. ☎ 91 725 18 57.

Telefónica: Fuencarral, 3. ☎ 91 522 66 45. Open from Tuesday to Friday, from 10 h to 14 h and from 17 h to 20 h. Saturdays and Sundays from 10 h to 14 h. Mondays closed.

Templo de Debod: Ferraz, s/n. ☎ 91 365 93 36.

Tifológico (Museo para Ver y Tocar) de la ONCE: Coruña, 18. ☎ 91 589 42 00.

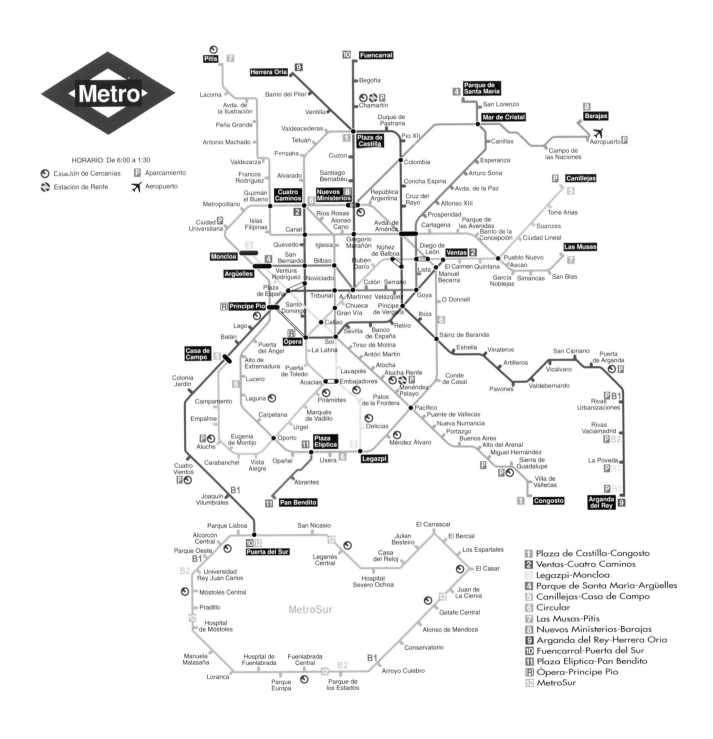

Metro

HORARIO: De 6:00 a 1:30

Estación de Cercanías
Estación de Renfe
Aparcamiento
Aeropuerto

1 Plaza de Castilla-Congosto
2 Ventas-Cuatro Caminos
3 Legazpi-Moncloa
4 Parque de Santa María-Argüelles
5 Canillejas-Casa de Campo
6 Circular
7 Las Musas-Pitis
8 Nuevos Ministerios-Barajas
9 Arganda del Rey-Herrera Oria
10 Fuencarral-Puerta del Sur
11 Plaza Elíptica-Pan Bendito
R Ópera-Príncipe Pío
12 MetroSur

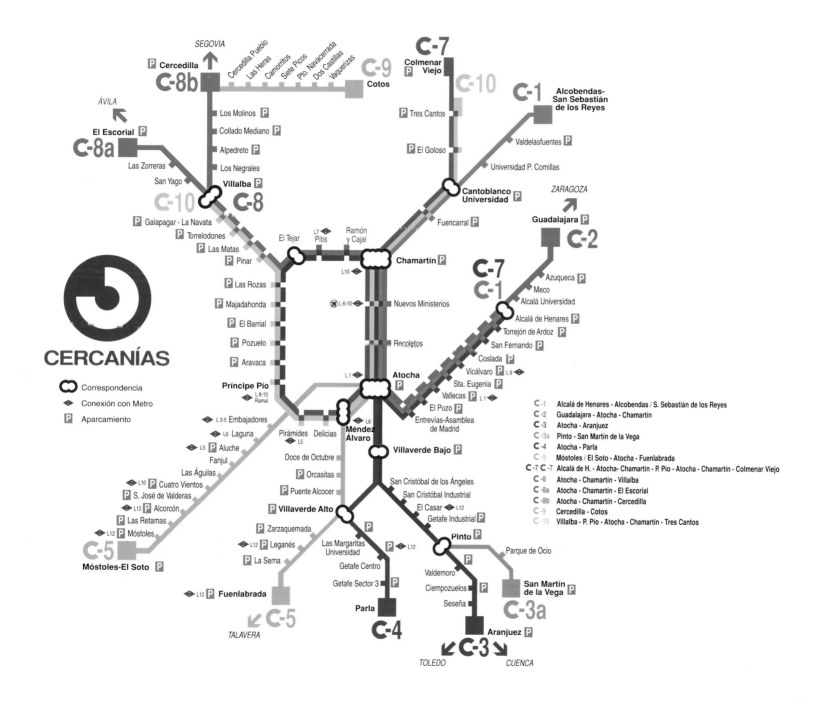

CERCANÍAS

◯ Correspondencia
◆ Conexión con Metro
P Aparcamiento

C-1 Alcalá de Henares - Alcobendas / S. Sebastián de los Reyes
C-2 Guadalajara - Atocha - Chamartín
C-3 Atocha - Aranjuez
C-3a Pinto - San Martín de la Vega
C-4 Atocha - Parla
C-5 Móstoles / El Soto - Atocha - Fuenlabrada
C-7 C-7 Alcalá de H. - Atocha- Chamartín - P. Pío - Atocha - Chamartín - Colmenar Viejo
C-8 Atocha - Chamartín - Villalba
C-8a Atocha - Chamartín - El Escorial
C-8b Atocha - Chamartín - Cercedilla
C-9 Cercedilla - Cotos
C-10 Villalba - P. Pío - Atocha - Chamartín - Tres Cantos